Boundless Vows, Endless Practice

Bodhisattva Vows in the 21st Century

BOUNDLESS VOWS, ENDLESS PRACTICE

Bodhisattva Vows in the 21st Century

SHŌHAKU OKUMURA

SHŌDŌ SPRING   SHŌRYŪ BRADLEY

DENSHŌ QUINTERO   HŌKŌ KARNEGIS

CENTRE SHIKANTAZA   SHŌJU MAHLER

EIDŌ REINHART   KAIKYŌ ROBY

DŌJU LAYTON   JŌKEI WHITEHEAD

EDITED BY HŌKŌ KARNEGIS AND SEIGEN HARTKEMEYER

SANSHIN ZEN COMMUNITY

Dōgen Institute

2018

Published 2018 by Dōgen Institute

Authors retain copyright to their work.

Boundless Vows, Endless Practice
Bodhisattva Vows in the 21st Century

Publications Design by: Hōkō Karnegis

ISBN-10: 1986563286

ISBN-13: 978-1986563284

Editor's Preface

Right after my installation as Sanshin's vice abbot, I went to Oku-mura Rōshi with an idea: what if, as part of the events surrounding the 15th anniversary of Sanshin in one year's time, we published a collection of writings from my dharma brothers and sisters around the world? The Sanshin network is truly global, and what better time to show off the variety of insights and aspirations it includes? After all, as Okumura Rōshi moves from his current role as abbot to a role as founding teacher—a transition scheduled to be completed in 2023—these are the voices of the next generation that will be tak-ing up the teachings and practice of our dharma family and carrying them forward.

I also wanted the chance to partner with my dharma brothers and sisters on a meaningful project that would not only honor their com-mitment to the dharma but offer something in support of Western Zen practice and practitioners. Nine of them responded enthusiastically to the invitation to share their practice through this book, and Okumura Rōshi agreed to choose the topic and write an introductory chapter to set the stage. He asked us to consider the nature of individual and universal bodhisattva vows, take inspiration from the vows of those who had gone before us—including Dōgen Zenji and other early Sōtō Zen masters, as well as his teacher Kōshō Uchiyama—and to write about what it means to make and carry out our own vows in the 21st century. His own chapter includes material and translations never before available in English, making this project a learning and discernment opportunity for us, the authors preparing our offerings, as well as for you, the readers who are receiving and practicing with them.

The variety of viewpoints represented in this book is one of the things that makes it valuable. Some of us have been transmitted teachers for years and others have become novices only recently. Some speak and teach often while others are just finding their dharma voices. Some are experienced at writing for publication; for others, this is the first foray. Some of us use English as our mother tongue and for others English is our second or even third language. I have edited these chapters with a light hand, wanting to preserve the authenticity of our voices and modes of expression. It's my hope that if you've met any of us personally, you will hear our voices in your ear as you read our words.

HŌKŌ KARNEGIS
Vice Abbot, Sanshin Zen Community
Bloomington, IN USA
12 March, 2018

Table of Contents

CHAPTER ONE

SHŌHAKU OKUMURA

Original Vow and Personal Vow

Originally, the Bodhisattva (Pali, *Bodhisatta*), which literally means a person who has aroused bodhi-mind, referred to Shakyamuni Buddha in his past lifetimes and in his final life before attaining buddhahood. The Bodhisattva practiced the ten *paramitas* (perfections) for seeking unsurpassable awakening. In the Jataka stories, when the Bodhisattva named Sumedha aroused bodhi-mind upon meeting Dipamkara Buddha, he thought that, with his ability, it was rather easy to become a disciple of the Buddha, attain arahatship following the Buddha's teachings and enter nirvana in his lifetime, but he took the original vow (*purvapranidana*) to be a bodhisattva and seek Buddhahood, which takes a much longer length of time. Dipamkara Buddha gave him a prediction (*vyakarana*) that he would become Shakyamuni Buddha in the far distant future. The Bodhisattva practiced as all different kinds of living beings, such as a deer, a monkey, a king, a monk, a merchant, etc., for more than five hundred lifetimes and finally attained unsurpassable awakening sitting under the bodhi tree in Bodhgaya, and became Shakyamuni Buddha.

In Mahayana Buddhism, all practitioners who have aroused bodhi-mind, the aspiration for seeking awakening (*bodhi*) and helping all living beings as Sumedha did, are called bodhisattvas (菩薩). One of the definitions of a bodhisattva is based on the idea that ordinary beings are living pulled by their karma (業生の凡夫 *gossho no bonpu*), whereas bodhisattvas are living led by vows ((願生の菩薩 *gansho no bosatu)*. In the four bodhisattva vows, the original vow of the bodhisattva is clearly expressed, based on the Buddha's teaching of the Four Noble Truths. For all bodhisattvas, taking the four bodhisattva vows is the starting point of the practice on the path toward buddhahood. When we receive the bodhisattva precepts, we also take the four bodhisattva vows:

Beings are numberless, I vow to free them.
Delusions are inexhaustible, I vow to end them.
Dharma gates are boundless, I vow to enter them.
The Buddha's way is unsurpassable, I vow to realize it.[1]

These are boundless and endless vows. At no time can we say that we have completely accomplished all of these vows, at least within this lifetime. Therefore, our practice is also endless. For us, these general vows are directions toward which we need to walk, one step at a time. Based on these four vows, we need to take our own personal vows (別願 *betsugan*) as the Bodhisattva (Shakyamuni in his past lives) did in each of his five hundred lifetimes, depending on who he was and what he could do to help other beings. Since each of us has a unique personality and capability, depending upon who we are and the situation in which we live, we take particular personal vows.

In the first part of this chapter, I would like to introduce the practice and lives of Dōgen Zenji and other early Japanese Sōtō Zen masters who were led by the original vow and their personal vows. In the second part, I would like to introduce my teacher Kōshō Uchiyama Rōshi's vows.

PART 1:
Early Japanese Sōtō Zen Masters' vows

DŌGEN ZENJI'S VOW

Dōgen Zenji's Hotsugan-mon

Some Zen masters wrote about their original vows in short writings called *hotsugan-mon* (発願文 a writing about arousing the vow). There is Dōgen Zenji's *Hotsugan-mon* taken from *Shōbōgenzō Keiseisanshoku* (Sound of Valley Streams and Colors of Mountains):

ねがはくはわれと一切衆生と、今生より乃至生生をつくして、正法をきくことあらん。きくことあらんとき、正法を疑著せじ、不信なるべからず。まさに正法にあはんとき、世法をすてて仏法を受持せん、つひに大地有情ともに成道することをえん。

ねがはくはわれたとひ過去の悪業おほくかさなりて、障道の因縁ありとも、仏道によりて得道せりし諸仏諸祖、われをあはれみて、業累を解脱せしめ、学道さはりなからしめ、その功徳法門、あまねく無尽法界に充満弥綸せらん。あはれみをわれに分布すべし。

仏祖の往昔は吾等なり、吾等が当来は仏祖ならん。仏祖を仰観すれば一仏祖なり、発心を観想するにも一発心なるべし。あはれみを七通八達せんに、得便宜なり、落便宜なり。

このゆゑに竜牙のいはく、

　　昔生未了今須了、

此生度取累生身、
古佛未悟同今者、
悟了今人即古人、
《昔生に未だ了ぜざれば今須らく了ずべし、
此生に累生身を度取せよ。
古仏も未だ悟らざれば今者に同じく、
悟り了れば今人も即ち古人なり。》
しづかにこの因縁を参究すべし。これ証仏の承当なり。かくの
ごとく懺悔すれば、かならず仏祖の冥助あるなり。心念身儀発露
白仏すべし、発露のちから罪根をして銷殞せしむるなり。これ一
色の正修行なり、正信心なり、正信身なり。

Along with all living beings, I wish, from this lifetime through many lifetimes, to hear the true Dharma. When I hear it, I will not doubt the true Dharma; I will not lack faith. When I encounter the true Dharma, I will discard mundane principles and accept and maintain the Buddha-dharma. Finally I will complete the Way, together with the great earth and all living beings.

Even though my past unwholesome karma has accumulated and there are causes and conditions that obstruct [my practice] of the Way, may all buddhas and ancestors who have attained the Way through the Buddha Way bestow their compassion on me and enable me to be released from karmic entanglements, and enable me to practice without hindrances. May their virtue and their dharma-gates (teachings) completely fill and pervade the boundless dharma world. Let me share in a portion of their compassion.

In the past the buddha-ancestors were like us; in the future we may be buddha-ancestors. When we look up at the buddha-ancestors, we see only one buddha-ancestor. When we contemplate arousing [bodhi-]mind, there is only a single mind that is aroused. When

*[buddha-ancestors] radiate their compassion in all directions, we
will receive helpful conditions and drop them off as well.
Therefore, Longya said, "If we have not attained the Way in past
lives, [we] should attain it now. Within this lifetime, we should enable
ourselves, that is, an accumulation of past karma, to cross over [to
the other shore]. Before they had yet realized the Way, the ancient
buddhas were the same as people today. When we attain the Way,
the people today will be the same as the ancients."
We should quietly study and penetrate these causes and conditions.
Doing so is direct acceptance of the buddhas' verification. When we
make repentance in this way, we will without fail receive invisible
help from the buddha-ancestors. With mind-thought and body-form,
we should make confession to the Buddha. The power of confession
melts the roots of misdeeds. This is true practice of single color; this
is the true faith-mind; this is the true faith-body.²*

One of the important points in his *Hotsugan-mon* is that taking
bodhisattva vows and making repentance are mentioned together.
Dōgen Zenji's vow is to complete unsurpassable awakening together
with the great earth and all living beings. However, even though we
vow to avoid making unwholesome karma and to create wholesome
karma based on our vows, when we look closely at ourselves, we
often see many things in our thoughts, speech, and actions—even
if they are small and subtle things—that might create unwholesome
karmic sequences that are harmful and defile ourselves and others.
Sometimes, we forget about the vows altogether and go in various
directions. Therefore, we need to practice repentance to continue our
bodhisattva practice. Repentance is our expression of our awareness
of the incompleteness of our practice. Then the power of repentance
cleanses us and encourages us to make a fresh start. We return to the
right track and continue to practice following the bodhisattva vows.

Another important point Dōgen Zenji mentions is the interpenetration of the buddha-ancestors and ourselves as ordinary and deluded living beings who have aroused bodhi-mind. The buddha-ancestors were ordinary living beings in the past and we, who are ordinary beings now, will be able to become buddha-ancestors in the future. Once we arouse bodhi-mind and practice, there is no separation between buddha-ancestors and ordinary living beings, samsara and nirvana, realization and delusion.

Dōgen Zenji wrote in *Shōbōgenzō Hotsubodaishin* (Arousing Bodhi Mind):

菩提心をおこすといふは、おのれいまだわたらざるさきに、一切衆生をわたさんと発願し、いとなむなり。そのかたちいやしといふとも、この心をおこせば、すでに一切衆生の導師なり。

To arouse the bodhi-mind means to take a vow that "Before I myself cross over, [I will] help all living beings cross over [the river between this shore of samsara and the other shore of nirvana]" and strive to [fulfill this vow]. Even if their outside appearances are humble, those who have aroused this mind are already the guiding teachers of all living beings.[3]

We don't arouse bodhi-mind to improve ourselves so as to accomplish something desirable for us alone. We practice to help others cross over the river between this shore of samsara and the other shore of nirvana. This actually means that we vow not to enter nirvana until all living beings have entered nirvana. We continue to work on the river to help others cross over. When all bodhisattvas work with this attitude, no bodhisattva enters nirvana. All bodhisattvas are working on the border between samsara and nirvana to help others. All bodhisattvas vow to be the last person who crosses over the river to enter the nirvana. If everyone is a bodhisattva, the other shore is empty; no one is there. This is a strange idea.

However, this is the essential point of bodhisattva practice. This means that there is no clear distinction between samsara and nirvana. One of the most important teachings in Mahayana Buddhism is that samsara and nirvana are one. Actually, there is no river between samsara and nirvana. When all people are working to help others on this shore, we find nirvana upon this shore of samsara even though we are still deluded ordinary beings and there are many problems and hardships. Actually, we are neither in samsara nor in nirvana; we are neither deluded ordinary beings nor enlightened buddhas. We are bodhisattvas working in samsara with all beings. We try to help dharma flowers bloom in the muddy water. Uchiyama Rōshi said that a bodhisattva is an ordinary being who is walking the path in the direction of buddhahood. When we arouse bodhi-mind and study, practice, and work with this attitude, we are not completely deluded beings, but we are not yet completely enlightened buddhas. We are walking on the path toward buddhahood, but we are still within samsara. This is the reason it is said that bodhisattvas do not stay in samsara because of wisdom, but bodhisattvas do not stay in nirvana either out of of compassion. In Mahayana Buddhism there is a concept of nirvana for this kind of practitioner: no-abiding nirvana (無住処涅槃 *mujusho nehan*). A bodhisattva is basically a "homeless" person.

Dōgen's Concrete Personal Vow

As an expression of one of his personal concrete vows, in *Shōbōgenzō Kesa-kudoku* Dōgen Zenji wrote about an experience he had soon after he began to practice at the Chinese monastery. He saw that the monks, at the end of morning zazen each day, held their *kashaya* (okesa robe) respectfully and placed it on the top of their heads, doing gasshō to venerate it and quietly reciting the robe verse:

How great the robe of liberation is!
It is the formless robe and the field of happiness.
Respectfully wearing the Tathagata's teaching,
I vow to save all living beings.[4]

He felt that he had never seen such a gracious thing. His body was filled with delight, and tears of joy silently fell and moistened the lapel of his robe. Then he took a vow to introduce Japanese practitioners to this practice. He wote:

ときにひそかに発願す、いかにしてかわれ不肖なりといふとも、仏法の嫡嗣となり、正法を正伝して、郷土の衆生をあはれむに、仏祖正伝の衣法を見聞せしめん。

At the time, I vowed to myself, "Although I am unworthy, by all means I will become a legitimate heir of buddha dharma, correctly transmit the true dharma and, out of compassion for the people in my country, I will enable them to see and hear the robe and Dharma that have been authentically transmitted by buddha-ancestors."

After returning to Japan, he made efforts to encourage his students to wear the authentically transmitted form of the *kashaya* (okesa) and each morning to venerate it and recite the robe verse. As the result of his vow and efforts, he wrote:

かのときの発願いまむなしからず、袈裟を受持せる在家出家の菩薩おほし、歓喜するところなり。

My vow at that time was not in vain. Now there are many bod-hisattvas, both home-leavers and householders, who have received and maintain the kashaya. *I am so glad about this.*

This is one of Dōgen Zenji's concrete personal vows. It has been continuously practiced for about eight hundred years not only in Japanese Sōtō Zen monasteries and temples but also many Zen centers in the West. To take a concrete personal vow (別願 *betsugan*) is to be determined to make efforts to accomplish something meaningful for the sake of the Dharma or beneficial for living beings within the situations we encounter. Not only did he introduce the okesa, but Dōgen Zenji also made tireless efforts to establish a community where people who have aroused bodhi-mind could practice based on the true Dharma and its authentic teachings following the style of the Sōtō Zen tradition transmitted by his teacher Rujing (Nyōjo). Dōgen said that he first introduced some practices to Japan such as *shosan* (informal meeting) and ceremonies such as the Buddha's Enlightenment Day celebration. In the *Shōbōgenzō* he described how to wash the face, brush the teeth, and use the toilet. In the *Eihei Shingi* (Pure Standards for the Zen Community), Dōgen described how a tenzo should work in the kitchen as a Zen practice, and how monks who receive the food prepared by the tenzo eat as a sacred practice of receiving an offering. In the *Chiji Shingi* he collected many koan stories about how monastic officers worked in their respective positions. He was not only a meditation teacher, a philosopher, and a poet, but was also a founder and leader of a spiritual community in which the members who had aroused bodhi-mind practiced certain concrete ways of living as the expression of the Dharma based on the Zen Buddhist tradition.

Vow to continue the authentically transmitted dharma

In Dharma Discourse 182 of the *Eihei Koroku*, Dōgen Zenji introduced a story of Shakyamuni Buddha in his previous life. In the story, Shakyamuni was a tiler. The tiler had a chance to encounter the past Shakyamuni Buddha, aroused bodhi-mind and took a vow to become exactly the same buddha. His vow was fulfilled many lifetimes later and he became the present Shakyamuni Buddha. This story means that the transmission of the dharma and its practice style from one buddha to another should be continuous without any deviation. Dōgen Zenji said he also aroused the exactly the same vow, and then he raised a question: "Does Dōgen also see the present Shakyamuni Buddha and the Buddha's disciples, and hear the Buddha expounding the dharma?"[5]

Dōgen's answer was "Yes." Based on Shakyamuni's teaching in the *Lotus Sutra*, Dōgen said, hearing the dharma teaching, accepting it with sincere faith and actually practicing it is nothing other than seeing the Buddha. Then finally he said:

"Furthermore, seeing Buddha's body with your ears, hearing Buddha's preaching with your eyes, and similarly for all six sense objects, is also like entering and residing in Buddha's house. Entering Buddhahood and residing in Buddha's house and entering Buddhahood and arousing the vow is exactly the same as in the ancient vow, without any difference."

Seeing buddha's body with the ears and hearing buddha's teaching with the eyes, etc, means that we are actually accepting and practicing the Dharma with our entire body and mind instead of seeing, hearing, ... and thinking about the Dharma teachings as an object that is separate from ourselves as the subject. Dōgen Zenji urges us to cast ourselves into the Dharma; then we are able to succeed to the Buddha dharma with our entire lives and our lives and the entire universe we are living in are the same as Buddha's life.

EARLY SŌTŌ ZEN MASTERS' VOWS AFTER DŌGEN

According to one of the biographies of Dōgen, entitled *Sanso Gogyo-ki* (*The Record of the Three Ancestors' Activities*), there were three dharma heirs who received transmission from Dōgen; they are Ejo, Sen'ne and Sokai. Although we don't have their *hotsugan-mon*, by taking a look at their lives we can see their personal vows.

Ejō → Gikai lineage

Koun Ejō (1198 – 1280) was two years older than Dōgen. Before he met Dōgen, he studied and practiced Tendai teachings at Mt. Hiei, then studied Pure Land Buddhism with Shoku, Dōgen's elder half-brother and a disciple of Hōnen, the founder of Jōdo-shū. Then he practiced Zen with Bucchi Kakuan (? - ?), a disciple of Dainichi Nōnin (? - ?), the founder of Nihon Daruma-shū. Dainichi Nōnin practiced Zen by himself, thought he attained enlightenment and established his own school. Since he was a charismatic teacher, his school became popular. Later when Myōan Eisai (1141 – 1215) came back from China after receiving transmission from a Chinese Rinzai Zen master, Nōnin was criticized because he had not received the credentials of official transmission. He sent two of his disciples to China with a letter of his understanding and asked that transmission be bestowed through the letter. The disciples visited a Chinese Rinzai Zen master, Zhuoan Dheguang (Jap., Setsuan Tokko, 1121 – 1203), in the lineage of Dahui Zonggao (Daie Sōkō, 1063 – 1135),

11

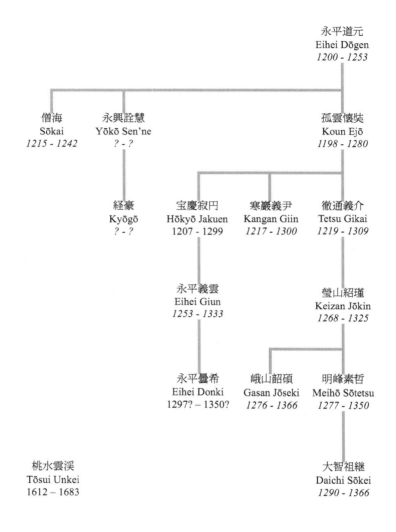

永平道元
Eihei Dōgen
1200 - 1253

僧海
Sōkai
1215 - 1242

永興詮慧
Yōkō Sen'ne
? - ?

孤雲懐奘
Koun Ejō
1198 - 1280

経豪
Kyōgō
? - ?

宝慶寂円
Hōkyō Jakuen
1207 - 1299

寒巖義尹
Kangan Giin
1217 - 1300

徹通義介
Tetsu Gikai
1219 - 1309

永平義雲
Eihei Giun
1253 - 1333

瑩山紹瑾
Keizan Jōkin
1268 - 1325

永平曇希
Eihei Donki
1297? – 1350?

峨山韶碩
Gasan Jōseki
1276 - 1366

明峰素哲
Meihō Sōtetsu
1277 - 1350

桃水雲渓
Tōsui Unkei
1612 – 1683

大智祖継
Daichi Sōkei
1290 - 1366

大愚良寛
Daigu Ryōkan
1758 - 1831

who strongly advocated *kenshō* experience through koan practice. Zhuoan accepted Nōnin's request, gave him transmission, and sent some Zen texts and buddha's relics as gifts.

Ejō had already received *inka* from his teacher Kakuan when he first visited Dōgen at Kenninji in 1227. After several days of discussion, Ejō recognized that Dōgen's insight was much deeper than his own, and he decided to become Dōgen's disciple. Ejō joined Dōgen's sangha at Kōshōji in 1234. In the first few years of his practice with Dōgen, Ejō recorded Dōgen's informal talks for himself to transform his understanding of dharma and truly become Dōgen's disciple. This record was found after Ejō's death, compiled, and entitled *Shōbōgenzō Zuimonki*. Ejō served Dōgen as his *jisha* (personal attendant) until Dōgen's death. He was always together with Dōgen, copying the manuscripts of *Shōbōgenzō*, and compiling Dōgen's dharma hall discourses that later became part of the *Eihei Koroku*. After Dōgen's death, he became the second abbot of Eiheiji and continued to copy and compile *Shōbōgenzō* and other writings of Dōgen. Ejō's vow was to accept and understand Dōgen's teachings and maintain his writings, in addition to continuing the monastic practice he established and educating capable disciples to keep Dōgen's lineage alive. Ejō gave Dharma transmission to several of Dōgen's disciples such as Tettsu Gikai, Eihei Gien, Kangan Giin, Hōkyō Jakuen, Gijun, Busso and so on. Among them, Gikai was the primary successor of Ejō and became the third abbot of Eiheiji. Gikai's successor was Keizan Jōkin, the founder of Yōkōji and Sōjiji. Keizan's lineage became the main stream of Sōtō Zen tradition. However, Jakuen's lineage and Giin's lineage also continue down to the present.

Sen'ne → Kyogo lineage

Yōkō Sen'ne (? - ?) used to be a Tendai monk before he became Dōgen's disciple. He was an eminent scholar. After Dōgen passed away, Sen'ne went back to Kyōto with his disciple Kyōgō (? - ?) and established Yōkōji (永興寺). At the temple, Sen'ne, Kyōgō and some other people continued to study the *Shōbōgenzō*. They made the first and oldest commentaries on the 75-fascicle version of the *Shōbōgenzō*. Sen'ne's commentary is called *Kikigaki* (聞書)and Kyōgō's is *Sho* (抄). When we speak about both together, the name of the combined text is Gosho (御抄). Yōkōji disappeared shortly after the deaths of Sen'ne and Kyōgō. The collection of their commentaries was moved to a temple named Senpukuji in Kyūshū. For several centuries, the text was stored in the temple without being studied, but in the 17th century, Sōtō Zen monk/scholars paid attention to their work and the Gosho became the most authoritative commentary used in the study of the *Shōbōgenzō*. It was considered the basis of Sōtōshu study during the Tokugawa period and has carried significant influence even into the modern age. Sen'ne and Kyōgō's vow was to study Dōgen's philosophical work in the *Shōbōgenzō*, make commentaries, and offer them to the later generations. They tried to make Dōgen's uniqueness clear in comparison with other schools of Zen.

Sōkai

Sōkai (1216 – 1242) was appointed the second head monk (*shuso*) after Ejō at Kōshōji. Unfortunately, he died when he was twenty-seven years old. Two dharma hall discourses offered in honor of Sōkai's death are recorded in the *Eihei Koroku*. In Dharma Hall Discourse 111, Dōgen introduced Sōkai's death verse:

Last night Sōkai (Sangha Ocean) dried up. How profusely the cloud and water monks have been crying! Although I see you [Sōkai] down to the [ocean] bottom, tears fill my breast like an overflowing lake. Yesterday I held up and shook the whisk for your spirit. With this one word upon your departure, I don't wait for you to revive.

And in Dharma Hall Discourse 112, Dōgen said:

Upon seeing this old monk [Dōgen], [Sōkai] did not have the same old face. While he was alive he never left the monastery. In the chill winds, while the fruits were falling, he transformed his thinking. A splash of water is his body; the clouds are his mind.[6]

It seems Dōgen thought Sōkai was an eminent person and expected he would make great contributions as his dharma heir. Had he not died so young, the history of Japanese Sōtō Zen might be different. We should remember that there must be many monks who died before their personal vows were fulfilled. However, their lives dedicated to the dharma are nothing other than expressions of the original vows of all bodhisattvas.

EJŌ'S SUCCESSORS

Tettsu Gikai

Tettsu Gikai (1219 – 1309) was originally a disciple of Ekan (? – 1251?), Ejō's dharma brother under Kakuan in Nihon Daruma-shū. When Ekan joined Dōgen's sangha at Kōshōji in 1241, Gikai and several of his dharma brothers also began to study with Dōgen. Gikai was a capable person. He served as *tenzo* after Dōgen and his sangha moved to Echizen; later he became the director (*kan'in*) of

Eiheiji. After Dōgen's death, Gikai visited various Zen monasteries in Japan and in China to study monastic practices and architecture to develop the Eiheiji monastic standard. After Ejō's retirement from the position of abbot in 1267, Gikai became his successor. Based on his research on various monasteries in Japan and China, Gikai worked on developing Eiheiji's facilities. Some scholars have suggested that Gikai moved the location of Eiheiji to the present place from the original location that was more remote in the mountains. While he was the abbot, there was some conflict in the assembly and Gikai had to resign the position in 1273. Ejō became the abbot again and served until his death in 1280. Gikai returned to the position of the abbot after Ejō's death. However, the conflict happened again and Gikai had to leave Eiheiji for good. He moved to Daijoji in Kanazawa around 1292. It seems Gikai's vow was to continue Dōgen's and Ejō's work of establishing Eiheiji as an authentic formal Zen monastery. However, he had some conflict with a group of monks in the assembly, possibly because of his double transmission from Ekan and Ejō. Keizan Jōkin was Gikai's main successor.

Gien

We don't know much about Gien (? – 1314), who became the fourth abbot of Eiheiji after Gikai left for Daijoji. A disciple of Ekan, he was from the Nihon Daruma-shū lineage and joined Dōgen's assembly. Gien served as *shoki* (secretary) while Dōgen was alive and he compiled a few volumes of the *Eihei Koroku*. He also worked on copying the *Shōbōgenzō* with Ejō. After he became the abbot and experienced some conflicts with Gikan, it seems Eiheiji had many difficulties and when Gien died, there was no one to take over the position of the abbot until Giun accepted the invitation.

Jakuen → Giun lineage

Another disciple of Dōgen who received transmission from Ejō was Hōkyō Jakuen (1208 – 1299). Jakuen was a Chinese monk. He practiced with Dōgen under Rujing (Nyōjō) while Dōgen was staying in China and served as manager of the memorial hall for Rujing at both Kōshōji and Eiheiji. After Rujing's death in 1227, Jakuen moved to Japan to study with Dōgen. After Dōgen's death, Jakuen left Eiheiji in 1261, practiced by himself in the deep mountains not so far from Eiheiji, and eventually founded Hōkyōji, which is still in operation today.

Jakuen's disciple Giun (1253 – 1333) took over Hōkyōji from Jakuen. After the death in 1314 of Gien, the fourth abbot of Eiheiji, Giun became the fifth abbot of Eiheiji. Subsequently Jakuen's and Giun's lineage maintained Eiheiji for several centuries.

年垂三八。自歎云。「金鱗合化龍。曷煩拘教網乎。」奮起更衣。
參寂圓和尚于越之薦福而服膺。圓常孤坐。淵默不屑誨勵。學者
無有合其機者。師自製發願文告其志於圓。其略曰。伏惟生死輪
轉之間生人間甚難。佛法流布之代遇正法最稀。浮木非喩。曇華
爭比。然而適投正嫡之室直修無上之道。聞未曾聞行未曾行。豈不
歡喜哉。是非小緣。正是大因緣也。乃至常啼東尋善財南訪。古尚
如斯。今可容易哉。觀之兮斷臂非難。念之兮燒身何辭。仰願此誓
約不朽至無盡未來際。乃侍左右採薪汲水苦行辛修殆乎二十年。

According to his short biography, Giun, the fifth abbot of Eiheiji, was a monk in the Tendai school. When he was twenty-four, he visited Jakuen to become his disciple. Jakuen was always quietly sitting by himself and did not give teachings as encouragement, so no one got along with him. Giun wrote his *Hotsugan-mon* and presented it to Jakuen to show his solid determination.

伏して惟みれば、生死輪転の間、人間に生まるること甚だ難く、仏法流布の代、正法に遇うこともっとも稀なり。浮木も喩えに非ず、曇華も争でか比べん。然れども、適々正嫡の室に投じ、直に無上の道を修し、未曾聞を聞き、未曾行を行う、豈に歓喜せざらんや。これ小縁にあらず、正に是れ大因縁なり。乃至、常啼は東に訪ね、善財は南に訪う。古えすら尚ほ斯のかくの如し、今、容易なるべけんや。之れを観ずれば断臂もうれいず、之れを念えば、焼身もなんぞ辞せん。仰ぎ願わくは、この誓約朽ちず、無尽未来際に至らんことを。

I humbly think that it is extremely difficult to be born in the human realm within transmigration in the circle of life and death, and that it is most rare to encounter the true Dharma. It cannot be compared with [a blind sea turtle] meeting a piece of floating wood [in the ocean] or with [the chance to] encounter an udumbara flower blooming [every three thousand years]. And yet, we are enabled to enter the chamber of the truly legitimate master, directly practice the unsurpassable Way, hear the Dharma we had never heard, and practice the practice we had never practiced. How can we help but be delighted? This is not a small connection; rather this must be [a result of] great causes and conditions [from past lives]. And also, Sadaprarudita Bodhisattva visited countries in the east and Sudhana traveled to the south. The ancient people were like that. How can we people today practice without walking through difficulties? When we observe this, we cannot worry about cutting off our arms. How can we refuse to burn our bodies? I respectfully hope that this vow will never wither in the endless future.[7]

Subsequently, he served Jakuen for about twenty years until Jakuen's death. In his *Hotsugan-mon* Giun expressed his gratitude for his fortunate life, not only being born in the human world but also encountering the true dharma that is beyond human karmic ways of life. It is really rare to meet a teacher who has received authentically transmitted dharma from an authentic master. That is much rarer than a blind sea turtle encountering a piece of floating wood in the boundless ocean or seeing an udumbara flower that blooms only once in three thousand years. Giun thought that this was a result of the great causes and conditions he had from his past lives. Because of this, he took a vow to dedicate his entire life to the dharma without avoiding any difficulties, as the previous bodhisattvas had done.

Sadaprarudita Bodhisattva (Jap. *Jōtai Bosatsu,* 常啼菩薩) appears in the 30th Chapter of *The Perfection of Wisdom in Eight Thousand Lines.* His name literally means "always crying." He was called by such a name because he was always crying at the sight of the suffering of all living beings in samsara. He took a vow to search for the perfection of wisdom (*prajna paramita*) for the sake of helping those living beings. In the sutra Shakyamuni Buddha said to Subhuti:

First of all, Sadaprarudita the Bodhisattva searched for perfect wisdom in such a way that he did not care for his body; he had no regard for his life; and gain, honor and fame did not interest him. He found himself in the seclusion of a remote forest, and a voice up in the air said to him:

Go East, son of good family! There you shall hear the perfection of wisdom! On your way you must not pay any attention to the weariness of your body, you must not give in to any fatigue, you must pay no attention to food or drink, to day or night, to cold or heat. You must not make any definite plans, either about inward or about outward things. You must not look to the left or right, to the South, East, West or North, upwards or downwards, or in any of the intermediate directions. You must not allow yourself to be shaken by self or individuality, or by form or the other skandhas, for one who is shaken by those is turned away from the Buddha-dharmas. When he is turned away from the Buddha-dharmas, then he wanders in birth-and-death. When he wanders in birth-and-death, then he does not course in perfect wisdom and he cannot reach the perfection of wisdom.

Sadaprarudita said to the voice:

That is how I shall act because I want to bring light to all beings, because I want to procure the dharmas of a Buddha.[8]

Thus he travelled to the East, and after experiencing various hardships, together with 500 women, he met Dharmodgata Bodhisattva and received the teaching of Prajna Paramita. One time he made up his mind to sell his body to make offerings to the Bodhisattva.

Sudhana appears in Book 39 of the *Avatamsaka Sutra* (*Flower Ornament Scripture*), "Entering the Realm of Reality." Upon meeting with Manjushri Bodhisattva, Sudhana aroused bodhi-mind and asked the Bodhisattva to give him guidance about how to study, practice, and complete the Bodhisattva path. Then Manjushri instructed Sudhana to seek genuine teachers and follow their teachings. He recommended that Sudhana go to the South and visit a monk named Meghashri. After that, Sudhana visited fifty-three teachers altogether, including monks, bodhisattvas, laymen, laywomen, gods, goddesses, and even non-Buddhists. The last teacher Sudhana visited was Samantabhadra Bodhisattva, who is the symbol of great practice. Sudhana's journey began with Manjushri, the symbol of wisdom, and ended with Samantabadra, the symbol of great practice. This story means that the ultimate wisdom (*prajna*) should be actualized in the practice that benefits all living beings.

Thus Giun expressed his determination to continue to practice seeking awakening and wisdom, and work to benefit all living beings without avoiding any difficulties. "Cutting off our arms" came from the story of the Second Ancestor Huike who cut off his arm to show his sincere determination to Bodhidharma. "Burning our bodies" came from Chapter 23 of the *Lotus Sutra*, "Previous Lives of Medicine King Bodhisattva." In his previous life he wished to make offerings to the Buddha Pure and Bright Excellence of Sun and Moon. After offering various kinds of precious incense, he thought, "Though I have made offerings to the Buddha with my divine powers, that is not as good as offering my body." He made a vow by his divine powers and set fire to his own body. "The light illuminated worlds as numerous as the sands of eight billion Ganges. The buddhas in those lands all praised him at the same time, 'Well done, well done, good son; this is true devotion. It is what is called a true dharma offering to the Tathagata.'"[9] It is said the bodhisattva's body continued to burn for twelve hundred years, after which it burned itself out. I interpret this "burning one's own body" as expressing or actualizing the Dharma through our activities using our body. Thus Giun took his vow to continue his practice, actualizing the Dharma through his body and mind and going through any kind of difficulty that may arise in the endless future.

Kangan Giin's lineage

Another person who received transmission from Ejō was Kangan Giin (1217 – 1300). It is said Giin was a son of an emperor, but we don't know whether his father was Emperor Gotoba (1180 – 1239) or Emperor Juntoku (1197 – 1242). In any case, both emperors were exiled by the Kamakura Shogunate after the Jōkyū War in 1221. Giin was four years old. Some scholars think Giin was one of the several monks from Nihon Daruma-shū who joined Dōgen's sangha; other scholars think he was a Tendai monk practicing at Mt. Hiei until he became Dōgen's disciple in 1241. After Dōgen's death in 1253, it is said that Giin went to China twice. His first visit was in 1253 and the second visit was from 1264 to 1267. This time Giin took a copy of Dōgen's *Eihei Koroku* and showed it to one of Rujing's dharma heirs, Wuwai Iyuan (Jap. Mugai Gien ?- ?) who made selections of less than ten percent of the original manuscript and wrote a preface to it. Giin also asked two Rinzai Zen masters to write afterwords on the collection. This selection was entitled *Eihei Dōgen Zenji Goroku* (*Recorded Sayings of Eihei Dōgen Zenji*) and was published in 1358 by Donki, who was the dharma heir of Giun, the third abbot of Hōkyōji and the sixth abbot of Eiheiji. That was one of the earliest publications of Dōgen Zenji's writings along with *Gakudō Yojinshu* (*Points to Watch in Studying the Way*), also published by Donki in 1357. These publications were also the expression of their vows to keep and make Dōgen Zenji's teachings available to the later generations.

After returning from China, Giin lived in Kyūshū and established a few temples, including Daijiji in Kumamoto. Giin's lineage and Daijiji temple are still in existence.

Kangan Giin's *Hotsugan-mon* remains today. It reads as follows:

参禅の漢は先ず須らく至誠心を起こし、清浄願を起こして、仏祖のみ前に於いて焼香し礼拝して白して言うべし。願わくは我れ此の、父母所生の身を以って、三宝の願海に回向し、一動一静法式に違せず、今身より仏身に到るまで、其の中間に於いて、生生世世、出生入死、仏法を離れず、在在処処広く衆生を度して疲厭を生ぜず、或は剣樹刀山の上、或は鑊湯炉炭の中、唯だ是れ正法眼蔵を以って、重擔と為して、随所に主宰とならん。伏して願わくは、三宝証明、仏祖護念。

People who practice Zen should arouse most sincere mind and take the undefiled vow, and offer incense, make prostrations in front of the buddhas and ancestors, then recite as follows: I vow that I will dedicate this body born of my father and mother to the ocean of vow of the three treasures. All of my movement and stillness will not deviate from the form of the buddhadharma. Wherever I stay, from this body in this current lifetime until I receive the buddha body, during the entire process, life after life, world after world, I will not be separate from the dharma, entering life and entering death. I vow to widely free living beings without becoming weary. Whether on trees of blades and mountains of swords, or in boiling water in iron pots or on burning charcoal in fireplaces, I will carry only the true dharma eye treasury as my heavy load, and actively work as a master wherever I may stay.

I respectfully request the three treasures to be the witness [of these vows] and the buddhas and ancestors to become my protection.

Giin wrote this *Hotsugan-mon* not only as the expression of his own vow, but also to request that his disciples walk in the same direction he was walking. He requested that they offer incense, make prostrations, and recite this vow in front of the buddhas and ancestors enshrined in the temple.

"I vow that I will dedicate this body born of my father and mother to the ocean of vow of the three treasures." This is the same as what Dōgen wrote in *Shōbōgenzō Shōji* (*Life-and-death*): "Just cast aside and forget your body and mind and throw them into the house of Buddha; then all is done by Buddha. When we go on following this [practice], we are released from life-and-death and become buddhas without using our strength or consuming our mind." This means as bodhisattvas we need to live being led by bodhisattva vows instead of pulled by our karmic consciousness that always seeks "my" personal satisfaction, even if that might be attaining some kind of enlightenment, escaping from samsara to enter nirvana, and becoming a buddha.

"All of my movement and stillness will not deviate from the form of the buddhadharma." "Movement and stillness" means that in all of our activities, whether we are quietly sitting in the zendo, working outside, taking rest or even sleeping, we keep mindfulness, being one with what we are doing here and now. "The form of the buddhadharma" is a translation of *hosshiki* (法式). Today this term is used to refer to certain sets of manners, forms or procedure in doing ceremonies, but in this case the term means the way buddhas and ancestors behave in their day-to-day activities and also the way they lived their entire lives.

"Whether on the trees of blades and mountains of swords, or in boiling water in iron pots or on burning charcoal in fireplaces"— these are examples of the devices used to torture hell dwellers. This means even if we fall into hell and stay there, we should carry the *shōbōgenzō* (true dharma eye treasury or true reality of all things) as the source of wisdom and compassion to express and share it with all beings. We should not avoid even going to hell; rather, we use any place or situation no matter how hard it may be, staying there as our practice place without escaping. "Actively work as a master wherever I may stay" is an expression similar to the saying of Zen master Linji (Rinzai): "In whatever place you are, you play the master [i.e., enjoy the use of each and everything]; every place you stand is reality (随処作主、立処皆真). When *vishayas* come, they will not be able to turn you [i.e., you will remain unbound by them]. Even if there were to be habit energy from previous lives, and even if there were the five karmas that bring on immediate retribution, leading to rebirth in the Avici hot hell, these themselves would constitute the great sea of liberation."[10]

This *Hotsugan-mon* is also known as Daichi Zenji's *Hotsugan-mon*. I am not sure why it is attributed to both Kangan Giin and his disciple Daichi Sokei. Probably out of his respect to the master from whom he received *shukke tokudō*, Daichi used this writing and transmitted it to his disciples. Daichi Sokei (1289 – 1366) became a novice under Kangan Giin at Daijiji when he was six years old. Five years later Giin passed away. Daichi visited various Zen masters in Kyōto and Kamakura and finally practiced with Keizan Jōkin. Then he went to China in 1314 and stayed there for about ten years. He returned to Keizan and later received dharma transmission from one of Keizan's dharma heirs, Meihō Sotetsu (1277 - 1350). He founded Gidaji in Kaga in 1327 and returned to Kyūshū. He founded several temples including Kōfukuji, and Shōgōji in Kumamoto Prefecture. His recorded sayings and other writings were all burned according to his will. A collection of about 300 of his Chinese poems and a few Dharma Words (Hōgo) still exist.

Kōdō Sawaki Rōshi (1880 – 1965) practiced from 1916 to 1922 at Daijiji in Kumamoto founded by Giin. After leaving Daijiji, he continued to live in Kumamoto until 1935, when he became a professor at Komazawa University and moved to Tokyo. Sawaki Rōshi respected Daichi Zenji very much and loved Daichi's Chinese poems. He gave lectures on Daishi's poems many times. One volume of the 19-volume collection of his *teisho* (lectures) is on Daichi's poems and Dharma Words (Hōgo). Sawaki Rōshi spent the money he received from the government as a pension for his military service to print copies of Buddhist texts, which he offered free to students and practitioners. He said the pension was not "clean" money, so he wanted to use it for the sake of dharma. On the back of the cover of those copies, this *Hotsugan-mon* was printed. When Sawaki Rōshi gave lectures, he always recited this *Hotsugan-mon* with all participants. Kangan Giin and Daichi Sokei's vow was an inspiration for Sawaki

Rōshi's practice. Sawaki Rōshi's vow was to travel all over Japan to promote Dōgen Zenji's just sitting (*shikantaza*), based on Dōgen Zenji's teachings. He called his teaching activities without a fixed temple a "moving monastery." Because of this, Sawaki Rōshi was called "Homeless Kōdō."

Keizan Jōkin's great compassionate vow not to become Buddha

Keizan Jōkin (1268 – 1335) was the dharma successor of Tettsu Gikai. In *Tōkokuki* (*Records of Tōkoku Mountain*, 洞谷記) attributed to Keizan, he wrote a brief biography of himself. He wrote, "When I was twenty-five years old, I took a vow to be a 'Great Compassionate Icchantika (大悲闡提)' like Avalokiteshvara [Bodhisattva]." (廿五 にして、観音の如く、大悲闡提の弘誓の願を発す。)

Icchantika commonly refers to living beings who have lost the potential to achieve enlightenment or buddhahood. A scholar interpreted this sentence to mean that Keizan took a vow to save all living beings, even including *icchantika*, the same as Avalokiteshvara. But according to the *Large Dictionary of Zen Study* (*Zengaku-daijiten*), this expression "Great Compassionate *Icchantika* (*daihi-sendai*, 大 悲闡提)" means that bodhisattvas such as Avalokiteshvara took a vow to be *iccantika*, that is, they never become buddhas because of their great compassionate wish to save all beings. As I wrote at the beginning of this chapter, since beings are numberless, when we vow to save all beings we also determine never to become buddhas or enter nirvana ourselves. I think this is a wonderful and powerful expression of the nature of the Bodhisattva vow. Keizan vowed never to become a buddha because of his wish to be like Avalokiteshvara.

In *Tōkokuki* there is an article by Keizan about his vows, written a few months before his death in 1235. This writing is difficult for me to understand, but it seems he wrote about a dream he had while he was practicing with Jakuen at Hōkyōji for a few years after he turned eighteen years old. Within the dream, he took two kinds of vows. The first is the general set of four bodhisattva vows to save all living beings, and the other came from his mother's request that he save women.

両願を発して曰く。生生世世、化度利生、等正覚に到るまで、乃至、過過遠遠の罪有り。微かも消する事あたはず。以って我が珍宝となす。諸の衆生を救済せん。別願一切、管らざるの是れ操行なりといへども、この両願は私ならず。

一願は、菩提心を生生に発して、本師宝慶寂円の所において、諸共に、慈氏菩薩の証明となすの故に、身命を顧みず、生生世世、本願の如く護持すべし。一願は、今世の悲母、懐観大姉、最後の遺言において、領納の発願、是れ亦女流済度の菩薩なり。敢えて欺くべからず。遺命に任せて、これを護持すべし。三世の諸仏、歴代の祖師、及び首楞厳教、一切の諸経、予が金剛の二願心を擁護したまへ。部ついに叶はば、必ず霊夢を感ずべしと。思念して打眠す」(原漢文。正中二年五月二三日の記録)

I took two vows and said, "Even though I will edify, save and benefit living beings, life after life, world after world, until I reach the ultimate awakening, there are many faults I have committed in my many past lives. I will not be able to erase them at all. I consider them my precious treasures. I will save all living beings. This is the practice that has nothing to do with all my personal vows. However, these two vows are not my personal vows for the benefit of myself.

The first vow is: I will arouse bodhi-mind in each and every lifetime and practice at the place of my original teacher Hōkyō Jakuen, and together with him, I will become a witness of Maitreya Buddha [the future Buddha to appear in this world]. Therefore, I will not hold dear my bodily life; life after life, world after world, I will protect and maintain the original [bodhisattva] vow.

The second vow is the one that was my compassionate mother's will as she was passing away. That is the vow to be a bodhisattva who saves women. I cannot deceive my mother. Following her final request, I should protect and maintain it.

All buddhas in the three times, all successive ancestors, Shurangama Sutra and all other sutras, please protect my mind of vow and keep it as hard as diamond. If [my vow] is in accord with the Buddha's will, I will without fail have a spiritual dream. So thinking, I fell asleep."

As Keizan himself wrote, he had a vow to save women. In the book *Sōtōshu Niso-shi* (*The History of Nuns in the Sōtō School*), ten names of female monks ordained by Keizan are mentioned.[11] He established a nuns' temple within Yōkōji for the nun Sōnin. A few nuns received Dharma transmisstion from Keizan.

Keizan had many disciples; among them, Meihō Sotetsu (1277 – 1350) and Gasan Jōseki (1275 – 1365) are important. Meihō took over Yōkōji and Daijoji and Gasan became the second abbot of Sōjiji. Gasan's Sōjiji grew into a large monastery with many branch temples all over Japan. This lineage forms the mainstream of Sōtō Zen down to the present.

CONCLUSION OF PART 1

In Part 1 I have written about early Japanese Sōtō Zen masters' vows. In doing so, my intention has not been to describe the history of early Sōtō Zen objectively and critically; I simply wish to introduce their vows as bodhisattvas. Some of them wrote about their vows, and others just practiced without talking about their vows. However, I think we can understand that all of the people I mentioned in this chapter lived and practiced led by bodhisattva vows, the four general vows and their concrete personal vows.

They lived led by their vows instead of being pulled by their individual karma, yet they could not eliminate their karmic attributes, such as personality, capability, or the situations arising from the environements in which they were born and lived in terms of time and space. They tried to offer themselves—including their personal karma—for the sake of establishing the dharma in their unique ways. Although they all took the same bodhisattva vows, their lives were unique. Therefore, there were some conflicts, separations and even factions among them. Their personal dynamics created the dynamics of the later history of the Sōtō Zen school. Our practice in the 21st century is still influenced by what these people did on the basis of their vows.

Until Keizan's generation, Japanese Sōtō Zen was a tiny group of monks. In the lineage chart in *Zengaku Daijiten*, less than 30 people are listed. After Keizan, the lineages of Meihō Sotetsu and Gasan Jōseki, in particular, grew and spread all over Japan. By the time the Tokugawa Shogunate was established in the early 17th century, the Sōtō school had become one of the largest Buddhist demoninations in Japan. It is said there were around 15,000 Sōtō Zen temples.

During the Tokugawa period (1601 – 1868), the Sōtō school was one of the major religious institutions supported and controlled by the government. When a religious institution is established, protected and controlled by a secular political power, often the essential spirit is lost. Some Sōtō Zen monks left their temples because of their vows. Tōsui and Ryōkan were the examples of such people who did not like institutionalism. Tōsui Unkei (1612 – 1683) was the abbot of a temple supported by a feudal lord in Kyūshū; after a summer practice period, he escaped from his temple. He went to Kyōto and lived with poor people who had become refugees because of the long age of civil wars. He was a homeless beggar or a day laborer. Ryōkan (1758 – 1831) is one of the most well-known Sōtō Zen monks in Japan today, but he never lived in any Sōtō Zen temple after he completed his training under his master. He lived in a hermitage in a mountain or a Shinto shrine in Echigo (Niigata). He lived by begging but is famous for his poetry and calligraphy. In modern times, the reason Sawaki Rōshi did not have his own temple was the same as that of Tōsui and Ryōkan. When he was a young monk, he found that even a temple can be an object of people's desire for fame and profit.

From the age of 43 until he was 56, Sawaki Rōshi travelled all over Japan teaching and encouraging people to practice Dōgen Zenji's zazen. Even after he became a professor at Komazawa University in Tokyo and the *godō* of Sōjiji monastery in Yokohama, he continued to travel until he was 83 years old. His vow was to promote Dōgen Zenji's *shikantaza*. Thousands of people, both Sōtō Zen priests and lay people, practiced zazen because of Sawaki Rōshi's continuous practice for almost 50 years.

PART 2:
Uchiyama Rōshi's Vows

I first encountered Kōshō Uchiyama Rōshi's teaching when I read his first book *Jikō* (*Self*) as a seventeen-year-old high school student. This book was a collection of his seven essays. The introductory essay, "A Note of a Way-Seeker (ある求道者の手記)" was about the process of his searching for the Way and his zazen practice. This essay made me wish to live like him and gave me the decisive influence of the rest of my life. In the first four sections of this essay he described the process of his seeking the Way, and in the final section he wrote about what zazen is and the significance of this practice for all human beings. He also wrote about his vow as a zazen practitioner.

I will summarize the first four sections to introduce how he sought the Way and translate the fifth section so that we can understand his vow. This essay was originally written in 1959 for NHK broadcasting and an announcer read it on a radio program. Uchiyama Rōshi was 47 years old, living at Antaiji with a few monks who were also Sawaki Rōshi's students and practicing zazen, and supporting his life by *takuhatsu* (begging) in Kyōto. He thoroughly practiced zazen in poverty, but he said he was satisfied in this way of life. He quoted Dōgen Zenji's saying, "Fulfilling the highest virtue with the lowest humble karmic body, within Jambudvipa and in the three worlds [of samsara], must be the highest virtue. (最下品の依身をもて、最上品の功徳を成就せん、閻浮提および三界のなかには、最上品の功徳なるべし。)"

Kōshō Uchiyama Rōshi was born in Tokyo, Japan in 1912. When he was 16 or 17 years old, he began to question what the meaning of life is and how he should live. He thought that his life was like a fresh blank canvas, and he wished to paint a painting with the theme "Living in Truth." Since he did not know what the truth was, he vowed to seek the truth of the self as a human being. That was his original vow, and he started his journey of searching for the truth. He further thought that at that time Japan was like an intersection of Eastern tradition and the Western culture that had been introduced since the Meiji era (1868-1912). Therefore, it was possible for him to study both the Eastern spiritual tradition of searching for peace of mind and the Western rational way of thinking, which pursues the progress of material civilization. He was inspired to create something new and integrated for the future of human civilization by studying both of them.

In search of the truth of life, he studied Western philosophy at the undergraduate and graduate schools at Waseda University in Tokyo. He mainly studied German philosophy. After finishing school in

1937, he became a teacher at a Catholic seminary in Oita Prefecture, Kyūshū, and taught philosophy and mathematics. He also studied Catholic theology because he thought that in order to really understand Western philosophy, he needed to understand Christianity. After six months, he gave up the idea of becoming a Catholic because he could not fit into its institutionalism. He also quit his job. He said that those six months were the only time he had a job and regular income in his entire lifetime.

In his twenties, he married twice. His first marriage took place while he was a university student. He contracted TB from his wife, who ultimately died of the illness. After coming back from the Catholic seminary to Tokyo, he married again. While his second wife was pregnant, she became sick and died after only a few days. This tragic experience made him take the decisive step to become a Buddhist monk to practice Zen under the guidance of Kōdō Sawaki Rōshi. Sawaki Rōshi gave him *shukke tokudō* (priest ordination) on December 8th, 1941, when Uchiyama Rōshi was 29 years old. That was the Buddha's Enlightenment Day and also Pearl Harbor Day in Japan when World War II began.

Practice under Sawaki Rōshi

At that time Sawaki Rōshi was the *godō* of Sōjiji monastery, one of the two main monasteries in Sōtō Zen Buddhism. Sawaki Rōshi borrowed a temple named Daichuji in Tochigi prefecture and let several of his disciples practice together as resident monks. They had two sesshins a month. Sawaki Rōshi visited the temple to lead one sesshin each month. In this sesshin, they had participants from outside the temple including lay practitioners. Activities included Sawaki Rōshi's *teisho*, services, work period, etc. In the other sesshin of the month, the resident monks practiced by themselves without the Rōshi. They actually sat all day. They repeated 50-minute zazen and 10-minute kinhin (walking meditation) from 2 am until midnight. They took turns carrying the *kyōsaku* (hitting stick to wake people up) each period. Only from midnight to 2am did they put aside the *kyōsaku* so that they could sleep sitting on the cushion. Uchiyama Rōshi said that after each sesshin his shoulder swelled up badly from being hit with the *kyosaku*. This sesshin was called *sannai sesshin* (sesshin only for residents in the temple) and this was the origin of the 5-day sesshin with modified schedule that was also called *sannai sesshin* which Uchiyama Rōshi started when he became the abbot of Antaiji.

His life completely changed when he became a monk. Before that, he was an intellectual person. Philosophical thinking and reading books were the only things he had been doing. Since he was from a rich family, he had never even washed his handkerchief by himself. He started to practice using his body and mind with strong determination. He felt very refreshed and delighted about that change even though it was extremely hard practice, particularly for a person like him who was highly intellectual and physically weak.

Sawaki Rōshi's disciples had to leave Daichuji after three years because school children evacuated from Tokyo came to live in the temple buildings. In 1944, Uchiyama Rōshi went to a place deep in the mountains of Shimane Prefecture to make charcoal during the winter, and then to a beach in Shizuoka Prefecture to work making salt. During this period he suffered from malnutrition. Almost all Japanese people were starving because of the war.

In 1945, after Japan lost the War, he moved to a temple in Hyōgo Prefecture. In 1948 he moved to a temple in Nagano prefecture, and in 1949 he moved to Antaiji in Kyōto. Since Sawaki Rōshi did not have his own temple and was always travelling, his nickname was

'Yadonashi (Homeless)" Kōdō. Sawaki Rōshi's disciples also had to be 'homeless' and moved from one place to another. But after moving to Kyōto, Uchiyama Rōshi settled down at Antaiji and lived there for 26 years until 1975.

Since Antaiji had no member families and no income at all, Uchiyama Rōshi had to support his practice by begging (*takuhatsu*). For several years after World War II, Japanese society was extremely poor. There were many real beggars in the city as his competitors. His life was really one of extreme poverty. By the time he wrote this essay in 1959, the condition of the Japanese economy was getting better, but living by begging was still difficult. Later he wrote an essay about his experiences while he lived on *takuhatsu*.

Not only did he have difficulties caused by poverty, but he also had to go through his own inner difficulties about zazen practice itself. After some years of hard practice of zazen, he found that he was not changed in the way he wanted before becoming a monk. He understood Sawaki Rōshi's important teaching that zazen is good for nothing, and therefore he could not complain. But then he had to question, what is the meaning of zazen practice? He was finally released by Sawaki Rōshi's saying, "Buddha Dharma is infinite and boundless. It cannot be something to fulfill your desire for satisfaction." Uchiyama Rōshi was entirely turned around by this saying at that time. He found that the wish to change himself and become free from desire for satisfaction was simply another form of desire for satisfaction. After that, he continued to practice zazen with the same hardships but without agony.

The following is a translation of the final section of the essay in which he explained what zazen is, the meaning of zazen practice in the modern world, and his vow.

Zazen as the Highest Culture
*(*坐禅という最高文化,「自己」２７頁*)*

What we experience in zazen cannot be truly understood unless we actually practice zazen. However, now I will try to explain the relationship between "the self that is always running around seeking the satisfaction of desires" and "the self that is immovably sitting and letting go of such thoughts and desires" by comparing them with "the clouds" and the "great sky above the clouds." I think this might be easier to understand.

Usually, we look up at clouds from ground-level using our eyes and think that the clouds exist high in the sky. Once I read a scientific book about clouds and found an interesting explanation. Suppose that we draw a circle with a 20-cm radius using a compass and consider this circle to be the planet Earth. The thickness of the atmosphere is only about the width of the line drawn by the pencil. Within the atmosphere, clouds are freely appearing and disappearing, and floating here and there. Clouds are such tiny things compared to the size of the earth.

Rain happens only below the clouds, but when it rains continuously for many days in the rainy season, we living beings on the earth feel like the entire sky is clouds and rain. The thickness of the atmosphere is only like the width of the line drawn with a pencil. Although above the line the sky is always blue and the sun is shining, unfortunately we are tiny beings who cannot understand this reality.

In precisely the same way, we are always covered by the dark clouds of sadness and agony, involved in the storm caused by anger or ambition, or disturbed by the long-lasting rainfall of anguish and despair. From our point of view on the earth, we have an illusion and are apt to think that all of heaven and earth are covered by the dark clouds, that we are attacked by a storm or that we are confined indoors by a long rainfall.

However, such "clouds or rain of thinking" is actually happening only within the atmosphere as thin as the line drawn by a pencil, or one even thinner. What I mean is that this is only happening within our thinking that is intent on seeking satisfaction. Outside of such thinking aimed at seeking satisfaction, there is no problem—the sky is blue, the sun is shining. Therefore, if we can sit immovably within this great sky, no matter how much rain of suffering and sadness we have to go through, we can see that the rain is also good, without becoming panicked and making a fuss. We can be stable enough to see such conditions simply as scenery that is coming and going.

Zazen is exactly like this. Even though all different kinds of thoughts are coming and going like clouds floating this way or that in the sky, we sit in the posture of letting go of all of them in the absolute stability of our minds just like the great sky.

Therefore, as a result of zazen practice, we cannot expect that poor people will become rich, or that we can be free of suffering even in poverty. No matter how much we practice zazen, poverty is poverty and suffering is suffering. Yet at the same time we don't have to think suffering has a fixed self-nature and is absolutely and always suffering. We are like the great sky abiding in absolute stability [although all different kinds of things are happening in our zazen.]

Needless to say, we cannot expect our economic condition to get better or natural science to develop by practicing zazen. However, the ultimate problem we are facing is not only how much natural science has developed, whether countries are being governed well and whether people are becoming rich, but also more basically, how the self can settle down and be at peace as the true self.

If human society is like rice grains stored in a container, simply a collection of human beings, it might be possible merely by governing skillfully in politics or inventing convenient devices through technology for us to cook the rice (human beings) into "happiness."

SHŌHAKU OKUMURA

However, human society is not like a collection of rice grains in a container. Each and every one of us (the self) in the society has a fang of desire for satisfaction like that of a wolf. This is the problem. And so, if there is a way to improve human society more fundamentally, it must be the way each one of us as the self can sit peacefully as the true self.

So simply by practicing zazen immovably and peacefully as the true self, I am making the best contribution to the development of the society that I can. Unbeknownst to other people, my personal zazen is already reverberating throughout the entire society.

And yet, if even one person begins to practice zazen inspired by my zazen, we must say that this is really a great event. Actually, since the time of Shakyamuni Buddha, the seed of zazen has been transmitted from one person to another, one by one, and has reached the present day.

If seeds are sown in the ground during winter, there is no way they can germinate. Yet if a seed of true zazen remains somewhere in this world, when spring comes, the seed will certainly sprout and grow bigger and bigger.

At the time, one person's zazen influences other people and causes a chain reaction; their zazen is transmitted to more people and finally it will circulate to the entire society. Under these circumstances, for the first time, we can say that human beings will open the first page of a history that is truly humane. I have been practicing zazen with such a deep vow and faith, like a prayer.

If I say something like this in this world today, all of you may say that I am simply dreaming. However, aside from this practice of the self settling within the true self there is no way to make this society, in which ego-centered selves gather together like wolves, into a better place.

37

Trusting in this, I am begging on the streets of Kyōto even today. In the poorest livelihood, I am practicing a zazen that is the highest culture. I am satisfied in this way of life, and I think we have to continue to sit on eggs until they are hatched. This is the way Bodhidharma's descendants have been practicing.

Uchiyama Rōshi was practicing with a few people at a dilapidated temple, supporting himself by begging on the street, but he was embracing all living beings within his practice. He had a faith in the Dharma of interconnectedness in which his own practice penetrates and echoes through the entire world throughout time and space. From the second half of the 1960s, both in Japan and in the West, there was a phenomenon called the "Zen boom," and many Japanese and Westerners came to Antaiji to practice with him. But when he wrote this essay, he was truly an unknown monk.

Bodhidharma in Shōbōgenzō Gyōji

After Sawaki Rōshi passed away and Uchiyama Rōshi became the abbot of Antaiji, he published several books and became a well-known Zen master. In 1975, sixteen years after he wrote the essay and just before his retirement from Antaiji, Uchiyama Rōshi gave his final lecture there. He talked on the seven points of practice he had kept in mind while he was the abbot of Antaiji, wishing to transmit them to his disciples. The third and fourth of these points are about the significance of "living by vow." He mentioned that when he felt discouraged by difficulties, he found consolation and encouragement by reading the section in Dōgen Zenji's *Shōbōgenzō Gyōji* (*Continuous Practice*) about Bodhidharma's coming to China. The English translation of this lecture is included in Uchiyama Rōshi's book *Opening the Hand of Thought.*[12]

Dōgen Zenji's description of Bodhidharma's voyage to China begins as follows:

The First Ancestor in China came to the Eastern land from the West following the direction of Venerable Prajnatara. Considering his three-year voyage through the seasons of frost and flowers, winds and snows, and [other difficulties], he must have been more than miserable; how innumerable were the raging ocean waves that he had to go through under clouds and mist. [Despite those difficulties,] he was determined to arrive in the unknown country. Ordinary people who hold their lives dear can't even think of [taking such trouble].

This must have been his "protecting and maintaining practice (gyōji)" that was solely based on his great compassion and [his vow] to transmit the Dharma and save deluded sentient beings. He was able to do it because he himself was the self of transmitting Dharma and [he was living in] the world of transmitting Dharma.

He could live in such a way because the entire ten-direction world is itself the true Way, the entire ten-direction world was nothing but his self, and the entire ten-direction world is no other than the entire ten-direction world.

Which circumstances in our lives are not a palace? And which palace cannot be a place for awakening? This is the reason [Bodhidharma] came from the West in such a way. He had neither doubt nor fear, because he was the self of saving-deluded-sentient-beings. He had neither doubt nor fear because [he was living in] the whole world of saving-deluded-sentient-beings.

"He could live in such a way because the entire ten-direction world is itself the true Way, the entire ten-direction world was nothing but his self, and the entire ten-direction world is no other than the entire ten-direction world." According to legend, Bodhidharma was a prince in a kingdom of Southern India. After his master Prajnatara passed away, he sailed to China via the Indian Ocean and the South China Sea. Dōgen imagines how hard it must have been to sail such a long distance, probably thinking about it in comparison to his own voyage from Japan to China, which was actually much shorter. Even though it took him only about half a month, Dōgen experienced many hardships such as heavy storms, sickness, etc. during that voyage.

The reason that Bodhidharma could complete such a dangerous mission was that he himself was the self of transmitting dharma, and he was living in the world of transmitting dharma. This sentence points to the identity of the self and the world, in which the self is living based on the intention and vision the person has. When Bodhidharma took the vow and determined to go to China to transmit the dharma, he became the self of transmitting the dharma, and his world became the world of transmitting the dharma. Dōgen mentioned the identity of the self and the world through actions based on the Bodhisattva vow to transmit the dharma and save all beings. This is why Bodhidharma had no doubt or fear, even when he was faced with many difficulties.

"The entire ten-direction world is no other than the entire ten-direction world" means that when only the ten-direction world is there, there is no Bodhidharma, no dharma to transmit, no India and no China. All of them became the parts of the ten-direction-world. This is the same logic Dōgen uses in *Makahannyaharamitsu*: "Form is emptiness, emptiness is form; form is just form, emptiness is just emptiness." The self is the world and the world is the self, and the self is only the self and the world is only the world. There is no separation between Bodhidharma, the Dharma, and traveling from India to China. All things there are simply the scenery of the entire ten-direction world, the world of transmitting the Dharma.

Uchiyama Rōshi's teaching of living by vow and rooting it deeply became a great help to me after his retirement, when I had to practice without relying on him. This attitude toward life became the core of my practice. If I forget that what I do is a part of my vow to transmit the Dharma, everything I do will be in vain and a waste of time and energy. The structure of our life as the intersection of the "universal self" and the "individual self" is also the source of compassion and the foundation of the bodhisattva vow to help all living beings including ourselves. It allows me to live without too much doubt and fear. All different kinds of thoughts coming and going underneath the clouds are not something we have to fight against and eliminate. Although thoughts are illusive, the human ability to see things that are not in front of us here and now and generate such fictitious thoughts is nothing other than the function of the universal life force. We see illusion as illusion and delusion as delusion, and then we are able to live without overwhelmed by them. There is no clear distinction between being above the clouds and being underneath the clouds. The universe is completely one wherein all different seemingly individual things are coming and going, appearing and disappearing.

This structure of our life is the foundation of the bodhisattva vow. When we see the universal self from the point of view of the individual self, we are inspired to live together with all beings in accordance with the universal life force. When we see the ego-centered individual self from the point of view of the universal self, we cannot help but repent of our unwholesome self-centered actions. When we awaken to this reality of our lives we cannot avoid arousing bodhi-mind, taking bodhisattva vows and making an effort to live in accordance with them.

Finally, in his last talk Uchiyama Rōshi said, "Because I believe vow is so important, I made it a rule to chant only the four bodhisattva vows before and after my talks. There's no need to argue difficult philosophical matters. Just hold these four vows; they're essential."[13]

In that final lecture, he said that he had two personal vows. One was to produce committed practitioners of strong zazen practice who could be models of that practice. The other was to write texts about zazen practice as the buddhadharma taught by Dōgen Zenji suitable for modern people. There are many Zen texts written in Chinese or Japanese, but they are all written in classic language using ancient concepts, expressions, and logic. He vowed to write understandable texts about Zen for modern people, both Japanese and Westerners. This is what he could do having studied Western philosophy, Christianity and Buddhism, and thoroughly practiced zazen. Thus the vow he took as a teenager to build a bridge between Eastern spiritual tradition and Western rational civilization was fulfilled.

Conclusion of Part 2

I inherit my vows from these two vows of Uchiyama Rōshi. When I finished at Komazawa University and entered Antaiji, Uchiyama Rōshi encouraged me to study English, and when he retired in 1975 he sent three of his disciples, including me, to the United States. Studying English and practicing with Western people became something natural to me. When I went back to Japan from Valley Zendo in 1981, he encouraged me to work on translating Dōgen Zenji's writings, as well as his own, into English. Practicing zazen with Western people and sharing the meaning of zazen practice and the Dharma teaching of Buddha, Dōgen, and Uchiyama Rōshi became my vow for my entire lifetime. I have been living by taking one step at a time. Since I am not an expert in the English language, I cannot make English translations without working together with native speakers of English. I have not been able to continue this way of life without the support, help, and participation of practitioners from many places, and I can only express my gratitude. My accomplishment of the vow is so tiny. We need many more people's participation to continue and spread the Dharma and zazen practice.

To do so, we need to work on a wide range of activities. I have been focusing my energy on just sitting and translating texts. I believe zazen is the core and foundation of all of the Sōtō Zen practices. To make the buddhadharma and the practice of zazen available widely, we need to do so many things, just as the early Japanese Sōtō Zen masters did based on their personal vows. I hope my disciples and Sanshin practitioners will continue to practice and work on the basis of their own personal vows according to their personalities, capabilities, and the situations in which they are living.

The former president of Komazawa University and current *seidō* of Eiheiji, Dr. Komei Nara, once said that transplanting a spiritual tradition to new cultural soil is like carrying an egg. The core of an egg is the yolk, but it cannot exist without the protection of the egg white and the eggshell. The white of the egg is like the culture of the society that supports the essence of the spiritual practice. The eggshell is like a system or organization that makes the framework in which the essential practice can be kept active in the society.

When a spiritual tradition becomes institutionalized and established in a society, often the essential spirit and practice is forgotten; it becomes only a cultural artifact, a rigid religious institution without vitality. This condition is like an egg without a yolk. On the other hand, when the yolk is without the protection of an egg white and a shell, it cannot survive. As Uchiyama Rōshi said at the end of his essay, we have to sit on eggs until they are hatched. To do so, we need to work on many aspects to form a new spiritual tradition in a Western culture.

I hope this collection of writings on bodhisattva vows can offer multiple ideas and observations as well as examples of actual practices the authors have been carrying out and inspiration for the future as we continue Dōgen Zenji's work in the 21st century.

NOTES

[1] This is the translation in *Sōtōshū School Scriptures for Daily Services and Practice* (Sōtōshū Shumuchō, Tokyo, 1873), p.74.

[2] Okumura's unpublished translation.

[3] Okumura, Shohaku and Leighton, Taigen. *Dōgen's Extensive Record,* Wisdom Publications, p.143-144.

[4] Okumura's unpublished translation.

[5] Conze, Edward. *The Perfection of Wisdom in Eight Thousand Lines and Its Verse Summary.* Four Seasons Foundation, San Francisco, 1973, p.277.

[6] Reeves, Gene. *The Lotus Sutra.* Wisdom Publications, 2008, p.354.

[7] Broughton , Jefferey L. *The Record of Linji: A New Translation of the Linjilu in the Light of Ten Japanese Zen Commentaries.* Oxford University Press, 2013, p.43

[8] Sōtōshū Niso-shi editorial committee. *Sōtōshu Niso-shi.* Sōtōshū Niso-dan headquarters, Tokyo, 1955.

[9] Uchiyama, Kōshō. *Opening the Hand of Thought.* Wisdom Publications, 2004, p. 161. I made some changes here from the translation that appears in the book.

[10] *Opening the Hand of Thought.*

44

Finding Home in the Vow

The Way is vast. We negotiate it, each of us, in the details of our own lives. Knowing these details to be unsubstantial, knowing the personal self as a phantom, still this is where we live. I write here about my own negotiation of the Way, hoping it may be helpful to others. Forgive me for speaking as if I had an independent existence.

I was an activist before any thought of being a Buddhist. When I wandered into Zen, this was the sentence that told me my place is here: "Beings are numberless; I vow to free them."

Before I had learned anything about Buddhism, before I heard of refuges or precepts or Noble Truths, the vow struck a chord in my heart. Of course, I didn't understand the deep meaning. What I understood was that my personal life was deeply engaged with the world around me—and that Zen affirmed my certainty of that. It was immediately clear that Zen was not about escape. I did not yet understand the matter of waking up with all beings, or how deep internal practice could be the way of freeing what I still thought of as others.

I had come cautiously to Buddhism, listening and watching for signs of hierarchy, of patriarchy, of anything less than complete freedom as I imagined it. Every teaching that set limits was a challenge for me—whether about forms, about anger, or about keeping the body still. But I was curious, and kept coming around. It was three years before my resistance changed—and that happened when I finally sat still long enough, surrounded by sangha and supported by a teacher. Things opened up inside me that I hadn't even known were locked. That entry to serious practice came at Rōhatsu sesshin, 1986, with Dainin Katagiri, Minnesota Zen Center, and Dōgen's "Painting of a Rice Cake." In that week, I realized that the world was alive in a way I had never imagined. A fierce eagerness arose, and I became one of those people who come to zazen every morning and attend sesshin every month.

That practice was driven by desire—the desire to live fully and to be completely who I was. There was no interest in being a Buddhist, although a wish to be a priest and a teacher appeared soon enough, and pushed me here and there. Somehow all of these carried me deeper and deeper into training and practice—first with Katagiri Rōshi, then in residence at Green Gulch Farm with Tenshin Anderson, and finally at Sanshinji with Okumura Rōshi, who welcomed me into the life of a Zen priest.

Looking at this history through the perspective of vow, I see these things.

The four vows are, as I think of them:
- to free all beings, to carry them across from samsara to nirvana
- to end delusions
- to enter all possible Dharma gates
- to realize the Buddha Way.

Considering my present desires in terms of the four vows, these thoughts come up—not in order of importance.

I want to live in the awakened world: to experience the aliveness of every thing and every moment, to lose the illusion of separation that was given me by family and culture. This want is actually the second vow: Delusions are numberless, I vow to end them. I want to realize this world as it is, interdependent, inter-creating, completely ephemeral and thus fully alive. I vow to let go of the dream of separation, the imagining of permanence, again and again and again, and to allow that lively universe to create me moment by moment. At first I wrote it this way: to go deeper and deeper into the stillness of sesshin, to go all the way in. But it's wider that that. It includes all of life, on or off the cushion.

I want to live the Buddha Way—really—to live as an expression of the life force, completely embraced, completely lived by all beings. This is the fourth vow: The Buddha Way is unsurpassable, I vow to (realize, embody, attain, become) it. It follows the second vow: Letting go of delusion, living in wholehearted life (the Buddha Way).

I want to offer the Buddha Way. This is the first vow.

Beings are numberless, I vow to free them. Literally, beings are numberless, I vow to carry them across to the other shore. I vow to bring beings from samsara to nirvana.

This vow exists at the level of illusion. In the Absolute, there are no sentient beings to be freed and certainly no "I" to make a vow. In the relative world, where we live every day, this vow is a way to relate to what seems like others. The first vow defines my relationship with the world around me, with every sentient being.

What is a sentient being? Science is gradually learning what Buddhism has always known, that "sentient beings" does not just mean humans, not even just animals—"sentient beings" means anything with consciousness. We do not exactly know who is included, though various cultures have thought they knew. Western industrial culture includes humans; some have excluded humans that were of different color or nationality; many primal cultures have recognized many more beings as sentient. I hold with those who include mountains, rivers, trees and forests, birds, fish and mammals, insects and bacteria and fungi as sentient. My vow is to carry all of them across from samsara to nirvana, and to arrive last.

PERSONAL VOW

At the beginning this vow had no words. I simply paid attention to what was happening in the world around me and participated in whatever way seemed possible. Always my intention was directed toward root causes, not toward simple alleviation of suffering. As a result, I missed out on the kind of direct service work that would have softened and connected me with other human beings. It's a personal loss, noticed only recently.

In my teens when I undertook to study physics, it was because I wanted to know reality at its deepest level. Years later I saw that Buddhism was the better place for that undertaking—but back then I didn't know. I remember applying for a summer student program, answering a question this way: "I want to understand everything, and I want it to be useful." Then, I had no concept of vow, but that was my vow. I couldn't imagine anyone—any real, living person—would understand it.

And that is why it mattered so much when I found the first vow. Here was a place where people understood. The more deeply I entered Zen practice, the more obvious it was that this vow was widely shared.

The early focus on causes persists. In addition, I am unable to think about sentient beings as separate; I can meet a person only in context. That context includes self, family, extended family, physical body and health, community including human and natural communities and the person's role in both, status including racial and economic status, personal history, and much more. When I think about that strange expression "freeing all beings," what comes to my attention is the broad spectrum of culture (including politics and much more), physical existence (including adequate food, safety, shelter, water quality), and an energetic level that I can't quite name. These items are influenced by my past as a psychotherapist, an energy healer, a social worker, a community organizer, an environmentalist, and an obsessive learner. I am impelled to address the collective. We live in a culture that glorifies greed, anger, and illusion, one that is destroying every kind of life on earth. This is where my work lies.

CLIMATE CHANGE

Perhaps fifteen years ago, I noticed in myself a vow to stop climate change. That's how it seemed to me: I never took that vow, just gradually realized it was there. I accepted it, and puzzled over how to live it out. I puzzled for a long time. I completed my formal priest training—during that time temple activities were an absolute priority, and in what time was left I studied permaculture, participated in local activism, had a bit of a social life, and earned a minimal livelihood. After leaving Sanshinji I committed to the first big activism that showed up—which was to go with the organization 350.org to the White House and get arrested there over the KXL pipeline. It was an attention-getting event—a successful one—but the ten days I spent there seem to have set something in motion.

In 2011 I went to Tassajara to complete the two training periods required before dharma transmission. In my first weeks there, during every period in the zendo pictures appeared—mental pictures of myself walking along that pipeline with a group of people. The pictures would not go away. I talked with practice leaders and with Abbot Steve Stuckey, and gradually came to the conclusion that I had to do this walk. There were another five months for it to cook—finding a name, contemplating direction, time—before I had access to the outside world. Okumura Rōshi said only "Don't do it until after you have transmission." 2012 became the year of dharma transmission—and of planning.

At some point during the planning, while I was quite overwhelmed, a friend asked me "What if you set that aside?" And the answer arose immediately: "For the rest of my life I would wonder what would have happened if I did it." I couldn't NOT do it, though it was extraordinarily difficult. While on the walk, called Compassionate Earth Walk, there was a certainty that whatever happened, I could not leave. And while I struggled, sometimes with my body, mostly with my co-walkers, I felt alive then in a way that has been rare in my life. (On return home, I collapsed exhausted for months.)

This is where I learned about vow: you absolutely couldn't quit. I had no choice but to finish the Walk, even if everyone else had left. It was a specific and tangible commitment, to walk from Hardisty, Alberta to Steele City Nebraska, with others, as a meditative and compassionate practice. Taylor, a walker in the first month, found a way to explain it to people: "It's a kind of peace walk." One newspaper article described us as protesting a way of life—because we insisted that we were not protesting the pipeline, and then we would talk about the way of life that destroys everything. People took us in, housed us, fed us, sheltered us, argued with us, taught us, and sometimes created situations where we could speak to local groups. Kai walked with us for two weeks during our hardest time and said as he was leaving, "You think you're not doing well. But you're doing something really amazing."

The original idea of the Walk was as a three-month-long ceremony, of relating to the powers of the earth as we walked through the middle of the continent. What actually happened, I don't quite know. I do know that in walking, one foot in front of the other, and placing the staff on the ground with every two steps, I could feel the connection. During the first month it felt like the earth was supporting this body and mind. In the middle I felt energy flowing from my feet into the ground. And at the last, it seemed as if both were happening together. Our walking together got quieter and quieter as the weeks went on. On the last day we only had five miles. So we walked slowly, silently, chanting the Metta Sutta silently in our minds. The thought came up, I wish we had done the whole thing this way. That actually means, next time do it this way. Next time, I will.

Afterward, people would ask what we accomplished. I could never answer. We walked. We stayed safe. With all our difficulties, we were a community. Every one of us was changed. That's what I know. Two years later, President Obama rejected the pipeline and people congratulated us—but it would be silly to take credit for that or to blame ourselves for Trump's reversal. We threw our offering into the stream, and it moved as it would.

In Zen morning service, we chant and then dedicate the merit, sometimes to a specific purpose or person, along with supporting the ancestors and all beings. This was like that. We walked for three months, increasingly in silence; there was zazen every morning, in cold or heat or mosquitoes; we talked with people who asked questions. We met whatever came up. I don't remember doing a formal, verbal dedication of merit, unless you count that last day of walking silently with the Metta Sutta. "May all beings be happy. May they be joyous and live in safety."

We had a closing circle the last night. The next day, I mailed the staff home before the Post Office closed at noon, and walked back to let the others know. Someone said "So it's over." The staff had been the symbol of the Walk, carried by each of us in turn, and the shared sense was that returning the staff ended the Walk. I said good-byes, got a ride to Greyhound, and arrived at 4 am in Burnsville, Minnesota. No problem that the bus station wasn't open; I napped on the grass and then watched a spectacular sunrise before my daughter picked me up and drove me home.

Before the vision of the Walk came up, I had not been clear about exactly how the vow would manifest. Afterward, the next step was perfectly clear: buy land, grow food, live in the country and do spiritual practice with all beings. So I began. But the instructions keep changing. At the beginning it looked like a farm and future community, and I plunged into learning permaculture-style farming while offering introductory Zen classes. Just two years later, the farm was mostly a place to learn how to be with other beings—a learning lab—and all my effort went to Mountains and Waters Alliance—an inter-species alliance, I said grandly. Things get turned upside down about once a year; I don't know what next year will bring, yet I must keep moving forward. Last year I took a rest from organizing; this year is for reaching out to others even though my own learning is still an urgent priority.

There are two aspects to this alliance. One is that climate change is moving ever-faster, and is already killing humans along with the escalating extinction of animal species and the devastation of plants and ecosystems, including oceans as well as lands. There are those who say it is too late; the one thing they haven't considered is that humans are neither alone nor lords of the universe. So I take that into account. Without crunching numbers or making predictions, I assert that our only chance is to abandon separation and join the family of life.

This requires me personally to do the work of abandoning separation. I look at the quackgrass choking out the garden plants and watch aversion rise inside of me. I pull out yet another baby apple tree destroyed by pocket gophers, and think about killing—and about the cruelty of killing—and ask for alternatives. Raised to think of everything else as a resource for humans, I despair of ever moving my own mind to that place where I can honestly offer alliance to trees, mountains, and bees. Yet they offer it to me. Sometimes they seem to speak, and I seem to understand them. This work is like walking blindfolded—and I propose to teach others to walk this way, even while I myself don't have it. And that is the second half—to free all beings from suffering, from samsara, from the illusion of separation and the greed and anger that result from it. I may say "changing consciousness" as the other half of Mountains and Waters Alliance; this is what I mean. Human beings becoming capable of allying ourselves with the rest of the world.

The fantasy arises that enlightenment would save me from these difficulties. Fortunately I know better than that. What is actually true is that all beings sustain me, and zazen helps me drop the illusion of separation. Zazen is the essential food for this work, for this personal vow.

ZAZEN

I mentioned an early recognition of the vow to free all beings. The other place of recognition was zazen. In 1983, visiting Minnesota Zen Center for no particular reason, receiving zazen instruction and sitting for fifteen minutes, it was there. I said to the instructor, "Can we do it some more?" and he said "No. You have to come back."

I did come back, and also sat at home every morning, wondering why people took the trouble to go to the zendo. My back pain lessened. Sesshin completely puzzled me, until at three years in, I finally sat Rōhatsu, seven days that broke apart the world. Those days showed me there was a living world outside the brittle structures of my ideas and opinions. Then I urgently began the process of breaking down the internal structures, wanting the whole living world to come in. It's still happening: "The sound that issues from the striking of emptiness is an endless and wondrous voice that resounds before and after the fall of the hammer." These words are from an old translation of *Jijuyu Zammai* (from *Bendōwa*) that we chanted at noon service during sesshin.

The third of those early learnings was bowing. This happened by accident. I had promised myself never to join a religion again, and was trying to avoid ceremonies. But I got caught, once, in those early days. The schedule said "zazen, lecture" on Wednesday evenings. But lectures were preceded by a service, chanting the Heart Sutra with three prostrations before and after. I found myself dropping to the floor like everyone around me out of simple conformity, embarrassed and slightly horrified.

The next time, the prostrations revealed themselves to me. I submitted to gravity, dropped to my knees, let the earth hold me in the pose of the child—and got up and did it again, and then again. Putting it into words doesn't work so well. But the bow brings this body from the independent, free, powerful standing place into the soft, intimate, relaxed posture that accepts the support of the earth. That was my second teaching. I held it close and private for a long time and finally was able to talk about it.

VOWING IS LIKE BOWING

In a wholehearted prostration, you begin by bringing your full attention and whole body into alignment.

Then you lower your body and touch your forehead to the ground. You may still have an idea that there's "my body" resting on "the ground," but you can't imagine independence any more while the ground holds you up. You lift your hands, on which Buddha is supposedly standing, elevating "the awake" above "my ego." And then you stand up again. You do something—another bow, chanting, or any number of actions appropriate to the moment.

This is one way we participate in the formal ceremonies of Zen, which are one way to participate in the world.

A personal vow is also a way to participate wholeheartedly in the life of the world. Both begin with being upright, with attention and focus, alert to everything around us. Both include letting ourselves be supported, by the ground or by the whole world. Both move from that awareness of support to a response, an appropriate action, in the ceremony or in the world.

In a prostration during a Buddhist service, the moment includes the community, includes a pattern of chanting and ritual actions shaped by centuries of tradition, includes your own body. You naturally move in the way brought about by all of these. In the vow, the moment includes the community of all life, including your personal or religious community. It includes the structures of life in the world, and the structures of appropriate response (ethical guidelines, precepts, *paramitas*). It includes your own body-mind-heart. Your motion, your action, is naturally shaped by all of these.

YOU CAN STAND ON YOUR VOW

The four vows create the landscape in which we live, the ground on which we stand, the terrain through which we walk. Each sentient being is a being with whom we have a relationship, not an object for our personal use. This one thing alone (and it is not alone) puts us in a different world from the civilization around us. The personal vow ties it to the specific life in which we live.

Okumura Rōshi names the difference between living by vow and being dragged around by your personal karma. This is important. It's not actually that I'm living by vow. Rather, the vow is a stable place, below and behind the movement of karma. Karmic fruit includes "I want to be important" and "Please, somebody love me" and "I want a break" even when there's wonderful work to do, or even when zazen is freely available. And it criticizes; it questions the vow and whether it is worthwhile, offers a thousand better alternatives. It offers the poison of self-doubt. Vow is stable, karma is chaotic, although sometimes karmic life is rigid, creating structures of addiction or compulsion to avoid life as it actually is. Seeking permanence—that's what I finally saw in that first sesshin: my structures and the fact that they were keeping me from life.

Last Tuesday I was at a talk by Ayo Yetunde (an Insight Meditation Dharma teacher) on the bodhisattva vow. There was discussion. Someone said it means preparing to die, and that seemed like the best answer. Then a response rose up in me: It means preparing to live. It means giving up the frozen unlife, the illusion of permanence and separation, and jumping into the dynamic stream of interbeing. The bodhisattva vow means being willing to live, allowing life to come forth through us, surrendering to life.

The Visible Form of My Vow

ALTHOUGH THIS IGNORANT SELF MAY NEVER BECOME
A BUDDHA, I VOW TO BRING OTHERS ACROSS BECAUSE
I AM A MONK.

EIHEI DŌGEN ZENJI (1200-1253)

After a deep life crisis that led me to give up my university studies, I joined the Teatro Libre in Bogota. As I was trying to earn
my living, I started reading on all kinds of topics in an attempt to
find meaning in my existence. In November 1984 a friend lent me
D.T. Suzuki's *Introduction to Zen Buddhism.* On one of its pages
I read these words of the Chinese master Shih-shuang (986-1039):
"Stop all your hankerings; let the mildew grow on your lips; make

yourself like unto a perfect piece of immaculate silk; . . . again let yourself be like an old censer in a deserted village shrine." I felt that Shih-shuang's description reflected a state of inner peace that I should pursue and that Zen was the path that would accomplish my search. I decided to travel to Europe and practice with the International Zen Association (AZI) founded by Master Taisen Deshimaru, who had died just two years before. I had some friends living in Paris who could help me find some means of livelihood. In late 1985 I was able to make the trip, but it wasn't until the middle of the following year that I got in touch with the AZI. Before doing that, I had had to solve the problem of how I would earn my living, which turned out to be quite difficult, especially since I lacked a work permit. Those were some hard months during which I had to confront my own relationship with the world. I was no longer living in the overprotective society I had left behind, since I was now living in a foreign country and had few friends on whom to rely. I had to get by on my own devices.

I started showing up at the Zen Dōjō at No. 17, rue des Cinq-Diamants in Paris' 13th district. I worked days and tried to practice earnestly in the mornings and occasionally in the evenings. Those were hard times but zazen motivated me to carry on despite the obstacles. I had discovered that the more often I practiced, the less vulnerable I was to outer circumstances.

In time I found some jobs that were a bit more lucrative and so was able to afford to attend some sesshin (intensive practice retreats). My early experiences in sesshin began to change the initial motivations that had led me to travel to France, because the experience in these intensive practice sessions went far beyond just sitting for a couple of hours. After that, each time a retreat was scheduled, I would make the effort to gather the wherewithal to attend. My new approach to zazen made me reflect on the direction that it was imparting to my life. Zazen was becoming an essential part of me, and I could no longer see it as just an activity. I felt the need to make zazen the pivot of my existence, and it was at that time that I made the decision to become a monk.

In November 1987, Rev. Roland Yuno Rech was leading an autumn sesshin at the La Gendronnière Temple and since I was planning to attend, I decided to request ordination from him. He asked me if I had received lay ordination (at which the bodhisattva precepts are taken), as that was the usual procedure. I replied that I had no time since I didn't know how much more time I would be able to stay in France, given that I was not in possession of residence or work permits. In addition, I argued that my wish was, upon my return to Colombia, to be able to start the work of spreading Zen, since in my country this practice was scarcely known.

Upon receiving his approval, I began sewing the okesa (monk's robe) and the rakusu that I would receive on ordination day. I was ordained a monk on November 1st, 1987.

Due to my illegal status in France, I had had several run-ins with the authorities that led me to think I would have to leave the country at any time. Yet one evening, through amazing coincidences, I got a phone call that saved me from having to make a hasty departure from France. Régis de Ramel, an elderly count and friend of a French woman I had met, was looking for someone to help him with some work at his chateau that was operating as a hotel. There at his place a range of different workshops on practices related to personal development and spiritual pursuits were being offered. The next day I made the trip to the south and visited the Château de Theyrargues, as it is called, located some fifty kilometers north of the city of Nîmes in the French countryside. To my delight, Régis hired me on the spot, and for the next year I lived at the chateau doing maintenance work, as well as taking charge of the kitchen. Thanks to Régis' generosity,

I was able to attend sesshins at La Gendronnière Temple whenever activities at the chateau did not require my presence. In the meantime I was allowed to use a small room at the base of one of the chateau's towers to set up a meditation hall. Sometimes several guests would join me in doing morning zazen practice, and so I was able to realize my vow to continue sitting and share my practice with others.

After a year at the Château de Theyrargues, I went to a small rural community in the French Alps to live, near the city of Montélimar. For several months I helped with construction work on a meditation hall and readying a house for residents. The community was located on the property of another close disciple of Master Deshimaru's, Laurent Kaltenbach. The practice at this rural center did not differ much from that at the Paris Dōjō. Aside from the fixing and maintenance work, we would practice zazen daily, mornings and evenings. The community work was hard and we rotated the kitchen duties. As in most Zen communities, all of us residents had to follow the established rhythms and schedules, working with everyone at the same time, and we would all sit zazen when it was time. In general, the rhythms of the farm were harmonious and we carried on a regular practice.

During the six months I lived in this community, I sensed there was a certain lack in my training as a monk. It seemed to me that I didn't have a real bond with the master who had ordained me as a monk, that the ordination itself was an empty formality, and that the continuation of the formal training process was quite dubious.

After several fruitless attempts to legalize my residence in France, I decided instead to return to Colombia, since the situation of immigrants was becoming more and more strained and my future quite uncertain. My thinking was that as long as there was a place and a zafu for me to sit on, the Dharma would remain vital in me. I knew that my practice would not be dependent on outer conditions being suitable, and I had every intention of setting up a practice center in Bogota and devoting my life to it.

After my return to Colombia in 1989, I started working on spreading Zen and set up a zendo with regular practice, days and evenings. I thought my experience from the previous years in Europe qualified me to organize practice. The group practicing with me soon included nearly fifteen regular practitioners and we organized some several-day sesshins. What I had not understood at that moment was that I had imported a zazen practice that was conditioned by my own limitations and a rigid outlook.

In spite of the scarcity of Spanish-language texts on Zen and Buddhism, I undertook a systematic study of the Buddhist tradition. I read up on the history and teaching so as to fill in the gaps I had in my training. I felt certain that if I couldn't have direct access to a teacher, at least it was my own responsibility to delve deeper into the writings of the tradition and the very teachings that had impelled the spiritual search of Master Dōgen. As a result of these studies, I started to write because I felt that this medium was a powerful tool for a greater understanding and sharing of my vision about this path. However, my first attempts at writing were riddled with errors and I found it difficult to get across to others what I wanted to say. I could not manage to use language in a simple and coherent way, but little by little I came to find the way to embody what I wanted to share.

At that time in Colombia an atmosphere of high tension prevailed on account of the terrorism spawned by the war on drugs. The assassination of Luis Carlos Galán, one of the candidates for president of the Republic most favored to win, along with the incessant bomb attacks, were creating an uncertainty and unease that were causing people to throw themselves with great yearning into a practice like Zen, yet I was not in a suitable position to give them what they wanted; I had no means of relieving their suffering. The style of zazen I had set up was imbued with severity, and that was not what people needed. My need was to find a place where I could continue my training and complete my education as a monk before attempting to help others. I tried communicating directly with the Sōtōshū Shumuchō, the school's administrative office in Japan. I wrote to its international section with the aim of having someone advise me as to how I could get in touch with a monastery in Japan to look into my options for admission and additional training. Despite the kindness of their tone, those I contacted always told me that for foreigners it was very difficult to enter a Japanese temple, and that in my case the best option was to contact the Buddhist Community in Spain. With much courtesy they sent me complimentary copies of the books that had been published up to that date by the Kyoto Sōtō Zen Center. These works had been produced by Okumura Rōshi, and since his address in Japan was included in them, I decided to get in touch with him.

From the very first time I contacted Okumura Rōshi, I tried to bring up with him my wish to travel to Japan and practice in a traditional monastery. However, on account of the issues of distance and my financial limitations regarding the travel involved, I never dared request concrete help from him, and so the prospect of a relationship was aborted before it even started. In spite of the difficulties, he assisted me by sending me a set of bowls so that I could go on carrying out the formal meal ceremony (*gyōhatsu*). I was deeply grateful and moved by his generosity. As for me, I continued reading and studying his works and publications, because I considered the clarity of his translations to reflect the essence of a Zen devoid of ornamentation, and for the first time I had access to writings by Master Dōgen.

Around that same time, another group based in Bogota brought to the country Zen Master Dokushō Villalba, who was leading the Buddhist Community in Spain. Following the recommendation of the Sōtōshu officials, I resolved to take advantage of the chance to talk to him during his stay in Colombia. During his visit he gave a couple of lectures and led an intensive practice retreat. In our meetings I had the opportunity to bring up with him the feeling that my training was still very incomplete.

Dokushō was an eyewitness to the harsh reality in which we were living in Colombia when a bomb exploded very close to where he was staying. He grasped the need that existed for establishing formal practice groups and was willing to welcome me into his Community. From then on, we maintained a frequent correspondence and together made plans for me to eventually travel to Spain. In the meantime, I collaborated long-distance with the Spanish Buddhist Community in translating texts from French and English and developing some topics for the Community's study program.

My study of the historical development of Zen allowed me to delve deeper into the way Buddhism has been transmitted throughout history. I understood that Zen as a school of this tradition resembles more a living plant than a cold doctrine. Zen has adapted to the conditions of fresh soil in which it has been sown, and in time it reveals some new traits more compatible with the people living in the place. I realized that in the future, Zen in Colombia would be somewhat different, but I also understood that this process was a slow one and that while this was happening, it was necessary to turn to the tradition so as not to go astray. It was incumbent on me then to carry on with some traditional training before attempting to create a new center in Colombia.

In spring of 1991, I managed to make the trip to Spain and practiced at Dokushō Villalba's Community for a year. However, things did not turn out as I was expecting, and because of family circumstances I had to return to Colombia, and my relationship with the teacher was broken off.

The experience in Spain, however, was very enriching. The chance to practice beside a teacher and follow a regular daily practice allowed me to enter a new dimension of Zen, much closer to what I wanted my life to be. It was a very special year during which I came to grasp more closely the meaning of sangha and the responsibility of my own work for the benefit of the community. The generosity of many of the members of the Spanish sangha deeply moved me: they really felt a deep appreciation for those who had devoted their lives to practice, and they had no qualms in sharing their space and their lives. I was witness to one of the essential practices of Buddhism—generosity. No wonder ever since the time of the Buddha, monks have been able to carry on their study and training, thanks to the generosity of laypeople. It is for this reason that in Mahayana Buddhism, generosity (*dana*) is regarded as a virtue, one of the ten "perfections" or spiritual qualities that bodhisattvas should undertake, develop, and attain, achieving its perfection to help others reach liberation from suffering.

Since my intention was to continue practicing and delving more deeply into my path of Zen, I went on seeking out teachers with whom to practice. In 1997 after having carried on a correspondence for several years with Rev. Tōzen Akiyama of the Milwaukee Zen Center, I was able to attend a sesshin led by him at Hokyoji in southern Minnesota. On that occasion I consulted with him about what I could do to validate my monk ordination, and he told me that he considered the person most suitable to guide me to be Okumura Rōshi, who was in the United States working for the Sōtō Zen Buddhism International Center in Los Angeles. I decided then to get back in touch with Okumura Rōshi and asked him about his schedule for that year. Because of the unavailability of much free time in my job and the fact that what time I did have did not coincide well with his schedules, I had to put off my meeting with him for several months.

Finally in May 1999 I managed to attend a spring sesshin with Okumura Rōshi at the Southern Dharma Retreat Center in North Carolina. When I met with him, I was able to express to him my deep wish to carry on my practice as a monk and, if possible, become his disciple. However, time constraints and the imposed silence during the sesshin prevented me from clearly laying out my situation to him.

Upon my return to Colombia, I had no other option but to continue my communication through correspondence and try to explain and demonstrate to him my wholehearted vocation. I made the most of free time between work hours to go deeper into my understanding of the Way, and I devoted myself to working on translating Kōshō Uchiyama Rōshi's book *Opening the Hand of Thought*, using Okumura Rōshi's English version of it. Among his publications, this book had impressed me very deeply, as I felt that it was very clear and direct with its particular stress on zazen practice.

Even though my vow was firm and resolute, there was a condition in my life I could not deny—fatherhood. I could not renounce my responsibilities toward my son, given that at that time I was his only financial support and we both needed one another's physical presence. The great koan of my life was how to live and train as a Zen monk while at the same time being a good father without neglecting my obligations.

Time was slipping away and I was not managing to find a way to fully devote myself to practice and to spreading the Dharma in my country. For me, being a monk was neither a certificate nor an objective in itself, but rather the visible form of my vow. It represented the embodiment of my years of seeking and my sincere wish to transmit a genuine practice. At that time my view of Zen practice had already undergone modification away from that ideal that I had when I first read Shih-shuang's poem. I no longer thought of Zen as a form of quietism for distancing oneself from reality. Quite to the contrary, it seemed clear that it should consist of a practice engaged with life. Indeed, it ought to be the purest manifestation of the life force. My work as a monk ought to be that of providing a space so that practice could be carried out. With this in mind, I continued to seek a way to surmount the obstacles that prevented me from proceeding with my training.

Around the year 2000 the violence in Colombia was escalating to an even greater extreme than in the years of my first attempt to disseminate Zen, and more than ever, I was seeing the need for promoting the spread of this practice. The fact that my ordination had not been registered with the Sōtōshu limited my options in carrying out this task. What's more, in some places priority regarding attendance at sesshins went to recognized novices, and such recognition was a requirement for participation in an *ango* (official training period) at training temples in Japan.

That same year, after some correspondence with Okumura Rōshi and getting an unpaid three-month leave of absence from my job, I traveled to San Francisco, where thanks to the generosity of the abbess at that time, Zenkei Blanche Hartman, I was given housing for the three spring months at the City Center founded by Shunryu Suzuki Rōshi. The idea was to be able to talk personally with Okumura Rōshi, who had moved to that city in connection with his work with Sōtōshū's International Section and was residing at that time at the San Francisco Zen Center. Right from the start, I brought up with Okumura Rōshi my wish to become his disciple. I handed over to him the translation of Uchiyama's book, which I had by then completed. I told him about all the hardships I had had on my road toward being able to accomplish my vow. Okumura Rōshi showed great understanding of my situation, but because of his living and work situation, it was at that time unworkable for him to take me on as his disciple. Instead, he encouraged me to go to Japan to practice at Antaiji and even wrote a letter to the temple head, Shinyu Miyaura Rōshi, asking him, if he deemed it suitable, to ordain me formally as a monk to help me continue my process. So it was that toward the end of May 2000, following almost two months in San Francisco, I shifted my plans and headed to Japan to practice at Sawaki Rōshi's and Uchiyama Rōshi's temple.

Miyaura Rōshi's capacity for work, kindness, and sense of humor opened the doors for me to a new practice. At Antaiji daily life was centered around zazen practice and communal work. From the first day of my arrival at the temple, I had to do farm work I was quite unused to, such as cutting down trees and moving them to be collected, doing garden tasks like sowing and harvesting, long days of weeding the fields while squatting, and the upkeep of the temple buildings and facilities. At the end of the day, the physical fatigue was very intense due to lack of habituation to these tasks, which were not hard in themselves but to which my body was unaccustomed. Even so, sitting in zazen in the evenings was wonderful at the end of these workdays, since the bodily fatigue was such that there was no need for worrying about the body, and as for the mind, given that it had been focused on the work chores, it didn't come to zazen with the vertigo that arises when one is idle.

The food I received each day had an enhanced value: I myself had worked on it. In the previous practice communities where I had lived, most of the work had pertained to construction, but now I was having to participate in agricultural tasks, the cultivation of foods that were the sustenance of the resident monks. Unlike many temples in Japan, Antaiji has no community of "faithful" that financially supports it, and its subsistence depends totally on what the residents can grow or on what they earn from the wood harvested from their forests.

On the intense workdays we sat zazen mornings and evenings, whereas on the first five days or the last three of a month, "toyless sesshins" were held. These intensive retreats consisted of fourteen zazen periods per day, practicing in total silence without anything to provide distraction, in just the way that Uchiyama Rōshi had set them up. They consisted of just three activities: eating, sleeping, and sitting.

At the end of June of that year, I returned to Colombia with authorization to go back the next year and receive monk ordination. From that moment on, my practice had a different direction. The chance to proceed with the training I had longed for for years had opened up for me, and the prospect of establishing a relationship with a teacher—something quite essential within the tradition—was taking shape.

The autumn of 2001 rolled around. It was only a few days after the attack on the Twin Towers of the World Trade Center in New York and amidst the uncertainty in the airline industry, I flew to Japan, ready to receive ordination. I arrived at the temple and everything went smoothly. My arrival at Antaiji started off with a sesshin. I recall one afternoon at just the halfway point in the five-day retreat; I went up to my room with some difficulty, as every part of my body was aching. The intense zazen periods facing the wall had brought up tensions in my knees, ankles, and back. My body kept putting up resistance to the prolonged stillness. There were still two and a half days to go before the sesshin would be over, and we were sitting for fourteen hours a day.

When I opened the sliding door, the pleasant scent of rice straw from the tatamis filled my nose. I opened the window to dispel the heat that had built up throughout the morning, and I stretched out on the floor. I looked outside and saw the stunning mountain that rose up opposite the temple. Countless cedars clustered next to one another blended together in varying shades of green. Dense horizontal streaks of mist were drifting across and blocking off the scenery. The two rice-paper screens were outlining this scene that I could view from where I was lying. Suddenly a white heron flew across the square I was gazing at, from right to left, and vanished with a squawk. The images of the planes full of passengers crashing into the Twin Towers came to mind, and I thought how absurd the world outside was. There was no other place in the world I wanted to be. On many occasions in my past I had wished to be in just this circumstance. Pain was no longer a threat, but had turned out to be a mechanism for revelation. It was now an ally that had allowed me to become aware of where I was. I understood how the preceding years had led up to this time. I had directed my life energy in such a way that what I was now experiencing would come to be: causes and their consequences, acts and results. And I felt fortunate. I realized that life—quite the reverse of how I had been thinking a moment before—was presenting me with a gift in the arising of a profound yearning. I was alive and awake, and in a few days I was to receive the monastic ordination I had longed for so much. On October 20th I received the formal ordination, marking the official start of my entrance into the Buddha's family. From that point on, I would need to follow my teacher's directions and help out at the temple to the extent that my conditions would allow.

A new twist in life, however, altered my circumstances again. In February of the next year, while he was clearing away snow from the road that leads to the temple, Miyaura Rōshi had an accident and died. On top of the sadness of having lost my teacher, my path had been cut off once more. I found myself again without the support of a teacher for continuing training and accomplishing the steps necessary for transmitting this practice formally in my country.

After Miyaura Rōshi's death, my search resumed. Thanks to the help of my friend Rev. Gakudō Nakamura, whom I had met in San Francisco, I was able on a couple of occasions to visit Shōgōji in Kumamoto, which offered a *kokusai ango*, a traditional three-month training period in accordance with the monastic standards of Master

Dōgen that was open to foreigners, lay or ordained and officially recognized or not. At that time I met Master Jisen Oshiro, who was the temple head. She was a short-statured nun but had a severe temperament that intimidated novices and kept them focused on practice. Her main concern was to help the participants acquire a proper practice, and thanks to her generosity, she served as a bridge for many Latino practitioners who were desirous of following a committed practice and getting formal training in Japan. As for me, though, given my circumstances, I was unable to remain in Japan.

In spite of the fact that the *ango* training at Shōgōji was not formally recognized by Sōtōshū, practitioners from all parts of the world were able to attend. Although given my time constraints I was unable to complete either of the two periods in its entirety, I was allowed to take part. Given these circumstances, I was able to savor the experience of training in a Japanese temple. I grasped the importance of the standards and the wholehearted devotion to practice spoken of by Dōgen Zenji. I understood that all the temple activities are formulated in such a way that it is essential to be focused on what you are doing and let go of parasitic thoughts that hinder the accomplishment of pure action. At the start, making mistakes is inevitable, but if practitioners get hung up on the error, whether it be to justify it or to stew in regret over it, they will get caught up in ideas of personal importance. It is crucial to understand that carrying out activities according to the temple standards is a tool for transforming the habitual tendencies of the ego. This involves forgetting one's own ideas of loss or gain and doing what one is supposed to do as part of the overall inner workings of the temple, without seeking a personal reward or acknowledgement. By doing so, the actions are part of the everyday activity of the collective community that operates like a fully integrated mechanism, in that each practitioner does his/her part. For years, thanks to the sponsorship of its head temple,

Zuiōji, Shōgōji has offered this three-month training free of charge. Most foreigners who were admitted as novices to Zuiōji were sent to Shōgōji to practice, and they would then become guides for the lay and ordained sangha who came to this *ango*.

While I was at the San Francisco Zen Center in 2000, I also found out that my friend Shōtai de la Rosa, a fellow practitioner while I was in Valencia, Spain, was practicing then at Tassajara, the mountain center connected to SFZC, and during the time I was there, we resumed our communication. Although that correspondence was sporadic, I found out from her in 2004 that Okumura Rōshi had founded a practice center in Bloomington, Indiana and that she had established a teacher-student relationship with him. That was how I got back in touch with Okumura Rōshi and began attending retreats at Sanshin Zen Community. Because of his close relationship with Antaiji, Okumura Rōshi was aware of Miyaura Rōshi's decease and Muho Noelke's being named as the new abbot there. Given Okumura Rōshi's new living conditions, he was now accepting students and ordaining novices. Since I was without a teacher, I once again brought up with him my wish to become his disciple, and just as in ancient Zen stories, upon my third request I was finally accepted.

Meanwhile, I started practicing with some friends who approached me for the setting up of a regular practice. We looked for a location and started meeting on Tuesday evenings to "just sit" silently. Little by little the group grew and eventually we had to seek a larger and more suitable place. In addition, we had to expand our schedule. In March 2006, thanks to the efforts of the group, we managed to bring Okumura Rōshi to Colombia, and several of the practitioners received the bodhisattva precepts from him.

The registering of my novice ordination with Sōtōshū and my relationship with Okumura Rōshi were the bridges that allowed me to get in touch with Dōshō Saikawa Rōshi, who was the official

Sōtōshū Sōtōshū representative (*sōkan*) for South America. From the time of his arrival, Saikawa Rōshi had committed himself to assisting novices in South America to formalize their ordinations. To establish contacts, his office had organized a sesshin at the beautiful Zenkoji Temple in Ibiraçu, Brazil, which I as well as novices from throughout South America attended. On that occasion Saikawa Rōshi offered me the prospect of doing a *hossenshiki*, the so-called "Dharma combat" ceremony. In December 2007 I underwent this ceremony at Busshinji Temple in São Paulo, officiated by Saikawa Rōshi and witnessed by my teacher Okumura Rōshi, the Brazilian teacher Coen de Souza Rōshi, several Brazilian monastics, and some members of the Colombian community.

Every novice is supposed to complete a certain period of formal training at a recognized temple, and so in September 2008 I requested another leave of absence from my job to attend the *ango* organized by Sōtōshū in France at the temple founded by Master Deshimaru, the same one where I had received novice ordination in 1987. The Sōtō School was opening up options to allow those novices who wished to get formal training but were unable to do so at temples in Japan to do it at these retreats organized and subsidized in the West. This retreat was the second one organized by the school and brought together 22 practitioners from different countries, sent by their teachers to practice in accordance with the same temple standards that Dōgen had established for his community in the 13th century.

As for me, my desire to attend the *ango* was not motivated solely by interest in acquiring certification as a teacher, but also by my interest in learning everything I could about the tradition and about Japanese monks. I had already tasted this practice at Shōgōji and I knew how important training was for becoming imbued with the essence of Dōgen's Zen. I was driven even more by the aspiration to share what I would learn with the people who were practicing with me in Colombia. From the moment I took on the setting up of a practice group in Bogota years ago, my chief motivation has been to awaken in others awareness that we all form part of one network called life and that whatever we do affects others. I was even more convinced that no matter what we do, if we fail to include others in our own practice, this practice will be meaningless. When the chance to attend the *ango* came up for me, I knew it was a unique opportunity for the mission that my friends and I together were trying to develop in Colombia. For me it was very thrilling to return to La Gendronnière, the temple where I had taken ordination for the first time 21 years earlier.

All during this period, Okumura Rōshi continued to focus on his work of carefully translating Dōgen's teachings and sharing them through his talks and writings. The more I delved into Okumura Rōshi's teachings, the more wonderstruck I was by the deep knowledge and intuition he had of Dōgen Zenji's work and by his surprising ability to share and make accessible these difficult writings that until then had seemed unfathomable to me. Gradually I came to understand the privilege of being able to study with someone who personified the two aspects of practice that for me constituted the essence: a profound devotion to the study of Buddhism and Dōgen's Zen, and an exemplary practice that was carrying on Uchiyama Rōshi's teachings.

In March 2009 I had the enormous privilege of receiving dharma transmission from Okumura Rōshi. Through this private ritual I was fulfilling my longtime vow to become a vehicle of the teaching, a bridge for other people to be able to benefit from this wondrous Way that was guiding my life. Actually, however, it was the start of a new phase in my responsibility towards the vow I had made to share my practice with others. My earnest aspiration was beginning to take shape thanks to the backing I had received from my teacher.

As part of my certification process by the Sōtō School, in August 2009 I visited Eiheiji and Sōjiji in Japan and completed the *zuise* ceremony. In this ritual the dharma heir who has just received a lineage officiates as honorary abbot for a day in each of these two temples. The first step is to pay homage to each of the founders, Eihei Dōgen Zenji (at Eiheiji) and Keizan Jōkin Zenji (at Sōjiji) in the Founder's Halls. The emotion I felt at that moment was indescribable, for I have a profound gratitude and admiration for the work that these masters accomplished. Thanks to their dedication and the fact that they were never stymied in the face of difficulties, the teaching reached down in time to me through my teacher. During the celebratory breakfast at the end of the ceremony at Eiheiji, I reflected on the auspicious conditions that had allowed me to find myself there. I recalled my first steps in practice, the times when from the bottom of my heart I had asked to be able to walk the Path, and all the obstacles I had had to surmount, one by one, to reach this moment. My gratitude toward Okumura Rōshi and toward all the masters of the transmission was boundless. This moment marked the beginning of a new stage in my path, a new dawn, a new beginning for practice.

At the end of 2009 I had the chance to attend a new three-month *ango* organized by Sōtōshu, to be held this time in California at Yōkōji in the mountains east of Los Angeles. This time fourteen novices from Europe, South America, and North America shared our practice amidst an extraordinary, isolated, and silent setting. There is a start to practice, but it never ceases. Every chance to practice in ideal circumstances like those of an *ango* is a great privilege and a transformative experience. It is a genuine opportunity to verify and express one's own understanding of the Way through everyday communal actions. It is for good reason that Dōgen Zenji said that as long as one has not practiced in an *ango*, s/he cannot be called a disciple of Buddha. The practice period is not a matter of chance; it is practice-realization itself.

In March 2011, I had the good fortune to visit Myōkōji in Kyoto, but the events that preceded my arrival at the temple would mark a decisive moment in my life. On March 11th at around two o'clock in the afternoon I was at Narita Airport boarding a plane bound for Fukuoka when the ground shook violently for more than two minutes, causing the catastrophic consequences that were broadcast on the news around the world. Immediately all arrivals and departures, whether by land or by air, were canceled. That night I, along with some three thousand people, had to spend the night at the airport, sleeping on the floor in sleeping bags supplied by the airport authorities and with blankets provided by the airlines. Nobody knew what was going to happen. Since I couldn't sleep because of the frightening news that was being broadcast on the giant screen and the continual aftershocks, I reflected on the dreadful experience that hundreds of thousands of people were experiencing at that moment and on how fortunate I had been, despite the uncertainty. In the morning, along with thousands of others, I boarded the train in Tokyo and finally managed to reach my destination in Fukuoka.

What astonished me most that night, and from what I could see in the subsequent days, was the impeccable behavior of the people. In the midst of shattering circumstances, amid the bewilderment from such an existential shock and having lost everything and not knowing the fate of loved ones, nobody was losing composure, no one was trying to take advantage of others—or even just advantage of the circumstances—for their own benefit. On the contrary, everyone was trying to help one another and get over their own tragedy so as to work for the welfare of the others.

During the time I was at Myōkōji, I was able to experience very intense practice within a completely Japanese setting. Neither when

I had been at Shōgōji nor when I had practiced at Antaiji had I had the experience of feeling illiterate. At this temple there was not a single person who spoke English well, and my competence in Japanese was only of a basic survival level. People would speak to me and I could hardly understand anything of what they were saying, but even when I tried to express some reply, not even hand gestures were of any use. I had the sensation that rather than having landed in a foreign country, I had woken up on another planet. Fortunately, the previous training I had gotten at the Sōtōshu *angos* and at Shōgōji had prepared me sufficiently to observe and imitate the other monks without causing annoyance in the rhythms of the community. The problem came when some type of explanation was required or people wanted to know something more about me. In any case, this experience of coming even to feel I was invisible at certain moments was very valuable for reassessing the idea I had of myself. One of the characteristics of formally entering a Zen temple is that no matter how many years you may have been practicing, no matter what your age may be with regard to the rest of the monks in training, no matter what credentials you may have achieved, on the day you enter you will be the last one in line. The position of your sandals will be farthest from the door, your practice spot the farthest from the heat, and your chores the lowliest. It is astonishing that with the exception of the resident teachers, one's personal achievements have no weight in the eyes of the community of practitioners. The monks immediately senior to you are over you all the time to make sure you are doing things properly. It is only when a new monk arrives that you shift in position at the temple.

Since the time of my first contact with Zen right up to today, my view of Zen has been undergoing transformation, and I am sure it will continue to be modified with the passing years. I have learned that obstacles are not barriers to advancing, but on the contrary are the fuel, the source of strength, and the motivation to keep us from being stymied by hardship or the fear of not being able to achieve our aim. The point where we find ourselves in the present moment is the result of all our effort and dedication—or perhaps the lack thereof—but most definitely the sum of the accumulation of circumstances that we have had to go through. The consequence of the decisions and paths we have opted for and everything with which we have become connected throughout our lives exists in us.

Despite my Sōtōshu certification as a teacher, I do not think of my training as having ended or of my having achieved something on my path. As Kōshō Uchiyama says, practice is lifelong, and my aspiration to create conditions for sharing this practice is growing day by day. I'm sure that through Zen practice and study, we can alter the behavior of our society—not through indoctrination or criticism, but through our example. Compassion, tolerance, and wisdom are the qualities that define this new form we have of connecting. Rigorous training, however, is essential for modifying our habitual conduct. It is important to study the example and teachings of those who walked the Path, as well as to carry out practice that obliges us to take responsibility for our actions and their consequences, thereby changing the impulsive tendencies with which we habitually react.

It has not been my intention here to present the stories of my life as an example for others, since I think that actually life itself, and not Zen, is each human being's spiritual path. Zen is the direction we follow, the northward point toward which we aim, the gauge that allows us to assess how awake we are at the moment of acting. If, however, our understanding does not manifest in our everyday relationships with those who are close to us or with everything we are connected with, then high-sounding talks or accumulated knowledge serve no purpose. I have resorted to language because I felt the need to capture in some way reflections on my experience in Zen, my years of trying to build an earnest and genuine practice for others. I have tried to abandon my biases and have allowed myself to mature through difficulties. All I want is for my daily life to be the expression of my zazen practice. In silence and stillness I endeavor more and more to take up the correct posture until such time as the conditions are present and my vow becomes reality. Only time and the wake that my practice leaves behind through my actions will determine whether I have succeeded in becoming a master teacher, even if it be only for a single follower.

CHAPTER FOUR

CENTRE SHIKANTAZA

What is a Bodhisattva?

Rather than writing a chapter himself, Mokushō Deprèay provides us with writings from his sangha in Belgium. He introduces the collection below.

When we started reflecting on this subject, we decided to draw our inspiration from Kannon, *She Who Hears the Cries of the World,* and to ask ourselves not what a bodhisattva is or could be, but rather what his or her action could be in a 21st-century world grappling with inequalities, violence, "ordinary suffering," and so on. How can the Buddhist teachings, the Four Vows, the Refuges, the realization of impermanence, and Indra's Net help us to act the right way in this world where suffering is ubiquitous?

We often hear that the devil is in the details, but it seemed to us that Buddha too is to be found in small things: in each loving thought, in each tender word, in each kind gesture we make towards ourselves and towards the world that surrounds us, in the care we take, but also

WHAT IS A BODHISATTVA?

in not looking away. As stated in *Tricycle's* "Daily Dharma" for February 2, 2018: "If you've taken a vow to save all sentient beings, it's time to go where the suffering is." You don't need to go very far to encounter suffering. It is on every street corner, in the look of this homeless man and his dog, in the sadness of this mother who knows she will soon have to take leave of her children, in the plight of the exiles and refugees who left their countries hoping for a better, brighter life. Suffering is in us too, each time we let our fears, our anger, our attachments, and our desires have the upper hand, each time we let our hearts shrink, each time we give in to discouragement.

Recognizing suffering, hearing it, letting it transform us and transforming it, being able to dive into it without letting it contaminate us. Keeping a clear and calm heart and mind. Giving the gift of "fearlessness." Reaching to others, not "from on high" but on an equal footing, one fragile human being to the next. All of these seemed vital elements in our reflection and in our approach on a daily basis.

Our contribution is divided into three short sections.

The first one, "Kannon is from Sudan," discusses a very topical subject in Belgium: the migrant crisis, or rather the crisis linked to the reception of the migrants who are fleeing war, tyranny, persecutions, or dire poverty in Africa and in the Middle East. This text shows how Belgian citizens from every origin, every walk of life, every religious and political background, decided to open their doors to these young people when the Belgian authorities were refusing them the most basic dignity and humanity. It also shows how, by doing this, the very same citizens experienced the opening of their hearts and saw their own world transforming.

The second text, "Mark," could have been entitled "Am I My Brother's Keeper?" The author answers with a definite "yes." How could things be different, knowing all of us are subject to impermanence and interdependence, and knowing every one of us is an equally important gem in Indra's Net, reflecting the light of all the others and having our own light reflected in all the others?

The third part in our contribution is a much more collective work from our small sangha. During a weekend retreat held in a Christian monastery, I asked the participants to seek, in their own history, an event, an encounter or an anecdote likely to fuel our reflection on the Bodhisattva Way and on the fifth vow as described in Okumura Rōshi's introduction. The idea was to make not a wish, but a vow in the form of a gatha, based on a genuine personal experience. The results of this work are presented here in the section entitled "Gathas for the Bodhisattva Way."

I hope you will find these texts helpful and wish you pleasant reading.

Kannon is from Sudan

Myōsen Leclercq

Making the beds for guests yet unknown,
I vow with all beings that we all go to the refuge.

Leaving the Palace

The first time I came in contact with "migrants" was in 2015. I'd read about this park in the heart of Brussels that had turned into a kind of camp harboring people from Syria, Afghanistan and Iraq, and about the volunteers who were helping them the best they could. I wanted to see things for myself. Once I arrived, I felt a very strong urge to turn back and run away. I realized I had been naïve, somehow convinced I would find a neat camping ground, full of "shiny happy people." I was faced with a slum full of meager, grim and distrustful-looking young men. Among them were a few people wearing bright yellow vests: the volunteers. I persisted. Breathed in, breathed out, "grasped my courage with both hands," as we say in French, and walked on. After a while, I started noticing a few coy smiles. A dark-skinned man with soft eyes approached, holding a plate covered with delicious-looking Moroccan pancakes. "Fancy a pancake? We've also got mint tea if you want…" I'd come to have a look, wondering if I could be of some help, and there I was, being offered pancakes and tea by the very people I meant to help. I pushed a bit further, along a group of women of North African descent handing out helpings of couscous, cakes and other treats. I found the tent I was looking for: the so-called "Ecole Parc Maximilien"[1]—an improvised kindergarten and school. Kids were playing in the yard. I went inside and saw a volunteer, a middle-aged woman with a broad smile. I gave her what I had brought: a game to help teach the children how to read and spell, coloring books, loads of colored pencils and felt-tip pens. "Oh, felt-tip pens! Great!" she exclaimed. "We're running out of them. You know, children keep forgetting to put the caps back on. And these," motioning towards a joyful flock of rowdy children, "are no different." No different except that the drawings proudly hanging from a handful of pegs told a very different story than the ones you would see in the average kindergarten classroom. A blood-red sea with makeshift boats loaded with crying people, a city with flames coming out of some houses. I smiled to her. "No, of course, they're no different." And I took my leave.

On the way back home, quietly crying to myself, I thought of the Buddha, how he must have felt when he had left his palace for the first time and discovered the suffering inherent in human life. I realized how, although considering myself a rather well-informed person, I had lived in a very safe "bubble."

THE BODHISATTVAS IN THE YELLOW VESTS

Flash forward. We are now in 2017. A second "migration wave" has arrived in Brussels. These people are still coming from Syria, Iraq, and Afghanistan but also increasingly from Egypt, Ethiopia, Sudan, and Eritrea. The volunteers are also back in their yellow vests, gathering as much food as they can to feed the newcomers, giving them sleeping bags, tents, warm clothes, and the like. But something has changed in the meantime. There have been terrorist attacks on French and Belgian soil. The army is still partly present on the streets and in the major railway stations. There is more fear and resentment among the population towards Muslims and dark-skinned people. The political climate in Belgium and the administration in place are also very hostile. Young men are arrested while queuing for a piece of bread and some soup. Some of them get beaten by the police (well, some of the police!), who take away the few things they own. They sleep outside in the mud, and are brutally woken up before dawn.

Then someone comes up with this new idea: We, the Belgian people, should give them shelter for a night or two, or more—a safe, warm, and dry place to sleep, in a bed, on a sofa, on a mat or even, if need be, on a rug. The idea gains ground. By the end of November a few hundred families, supported by several thousand others, are sheltering more than 300 migrants every single night. And every single night, a small team of volunteers stays up until the wee hours, shivering in the cold and the damp, trying to find a home for everyone. They post messages on Facebook every so often. "Come on, we still have some 30 extremely nice guys waiting… It's freezing cold out here. Pleeeeeaaaase!" "10 to go, come on, we can make it!" These people never seem to get tired. They all have jobs and families and still, here they are every single night, helping out of sheer humanity with humor and extreme kindness, with patience, with a thousand eyes and a thousand (smartphone-equipped) arms. The Facebook group organizing things has been growing fast and steadily (almost 21,000 members by November 30th, 2017). Some people offer shelter, others food or clothes. There are a few designated drivers as well, who bring the guests to their hosts' places, sometimes tens of miles away. "Guests." Yes, that's what we call the ones we don't know. What had started out as "I can have two migrants over for the night" has soon turned into "I have room for two guests tonight. Shall I come and pick them up or can one of you, dear drivers, bring them to my place?" Sometimes the message is "Has anyone seen my friends Such and Such? Their beds are waiting for them!" People tell their anecdotes (good and not so good)[2], ask questions ("Is it safe to bring them to the bus stop and give them a bus ticket for the ride back?"), help each other ("Does anyone here speak Amharic? A. is trying to tell me something Google Translate doesn't seem to understand...") share their tips and tricks ("Don't forget to put some hot chili sauce on the table; they just love it"), and give each other a hand. A student told how she would like to help but lacked the money to feed several people. An unknown woman turned up at her door with bread, eggs and home-made jam. There's a lot of love at work in this group. Helping each other seems like a simple, normal thing to do, "like a person in the middle of the night reaching behind his head for the pillow."

This is how we met Denis, Sandra, Catherine, Nicolas and Sabrina, all living and working in and around our small hometown and determined to help these mostly-young men and women build a future, taking care of the more vulnerable (some of the "migrants" are barely 14 or 15 years old). This is also how we met Sati and Ahmed, our first "guests," two young Sudanese men with radiant smiles, incredibly soft-spoken, discreet, and kind. They stayed with us for less than 24 hours, and still they left a lasting mark on our lives.

SAME AND DIFFERENT

Opening your home almost "out of the blue" to a complete stranger for one or more nights is quite an experience—someone you have not chosen, someone whom a volunteer, or chance, has assigned to you, someone of whom you know nothing. Man or woman? From which country? What background? Will he or she be joyful, angry, weary? Can I trust him or her? Of course, somehow, we all hope we get smiling, agreeable, and accommodating guests, people whom we will like and who will like us. The only thing you know is that they will be people who, by definition, will definitely not be "like you," coming from a totally different culture and background, having lived so many lives in this one life... People who, by definition, will definitely be "like you"—human beings who just want to be safe, free from suffering, who get cold and hungry, who need sleep, who have dreams big and small, who just want to be happy and loved. They have many reasons to be afraid of you because, after all, they don't know you, and they don't know if they can trust you. Possibly they are tired of changing homes every few nights, not knowing where they will be the next day, and not even knowing if they will find a roof at all... Can we really afford to be picky, considering this?

Some of these young men and women were hardly teenagers when they fled their country, leaving behind everything they had—a home and a family, if in fact they still had a home and a family to begin with. Some have been through hell before arriving here, and somehow they are still not exactly through it. Still, they are humans just like us. They can be more or less agreeable, just like us. Moody, just like us. Tired, just like us. Hopeless, just like us. Greedy, just like us. More fundamentally, they are Buddhas, just like us. Can you see the Buddha in every single person? Can you see each person as having once been your mother and father?

Can you see and treat them like this? Or at least try your very best to do so? I'm not sure, but I'm willing to give it a try. It is our minds that create these categories—friends, enemies, strangers.

These and other thoughts—fear, anger at our government for not taking care of them (probably a very European point of view), reluctance to be forced out of my comfort zone—flew through my mind as I kept on reading what others were doing and pondering whether we should welcome guests. But if we, of all people, did not, then who? And if we did not do it now, of all times, then when? So we took the leap.

SEPARATE AND INSEPARABLE

Before leaving, Sati told us, "I hope someday I can help you." Sati, there is something you need to know: you already did. You had even before you showed up at our door. You had even before you left Sudan. You had even before you were born. Of course, like so many others, we opened our door and helped two young people in need, but you presented us with this opportunity to give and grow, to overcome fear, to reach out of our comfort zone, to open up and unfold our hearts. By helping and deciding to trust you, we helped ourselves. By letting us help you, by being willing to take this chance and trust us, you helped both us and yourself. Not before, not after, at the very same time. We now are forever interconnected—as we have always been.

NOTES

1 This ad hoc school still exists, and it is still run by volunteer teachers. It is now hosted in a building in Brussels. On November 18th, 2017, a group of 20 Belgian teenagers from all over the country, aged 12 to 18, honored it with the first ever "Belgian Award for the Protection of Children's Rights." The formal ceremony took place at the Belgian Parliament.

2 A worthwhile read (in French): *www.perlesdaccueil.be/*

MARK

Myōsen Leclercq

I had been seeing them for a few weeks on market days. He seemed lost in his thoughts, grumbling from time to time when someone told him off or made a disapproving comment. She was snugged against his thigh, tucked in a blanket. Sometimes I would give them a coin or two as I rushed by.

Then one day, one freezing January day, as if by surprise, I realized I was thinking of them. Where were they? I thought that if I saw them next Sunday, I would give them something. Soup. Yes, soup! I'd give them a nice bowl of hot soup. It was so cold...

Sunday came, and so did they. I hurried home to prepare split pea soup. For once, I'd put bacon in it—lots of bacon. They needed it badly. Some invigorating, thick soup. Two large chunks of bread. A piece of cake maybe? Would that be too much?

My offering of soup was met with a wary eye. Then a smile. A "thank you." François—that's his name—eagerly opened the container. The smell of bacon woke Diane, the dog.

The week after, mushroom soup was on the menu. I squatted before him to meet him face to face. Diane did not mind being petted.

Diane and François came into my life without more than a gaze and a few words being exchanged. It's almost tradition now, wondering which soup I could prepare for them next Sunday and worrying a bit that they won't get any when I'm away.

For no known reason, some people touch our hearts more than others. Of course that's not fair. But still, that's how it goes most of the time. Now, I must admit I know why François's sight did touch me. Truth is—although I wasn't really aware of this in the first place—he reminded me of my godfather. My godfather, whose death I learnt of almost by chance. "Oh, by the way, Mark is dead." Mark? "Of course, Mark! Your godfather!" At the time I hadn't seen him in... 25 years, I guess. Mark died on the street, or almost so. I don't know all the details. He had been well-off, though. Mark was an engineer. He had a good job, a house, and a family. Then there had been that fractious divorce, putting an end to a married life that had never been a very happy one either. And a drinking problem. Had he taken to drinking before or after he and his wife split? No idea. All I remember about Mark is how gentle he was. In my childhood memories, Mark was a kind, bearded giant who always made me laugh. As time went by, his world had shrunk to the confines of his suffering, his only solace coming from the booze. He had totally, irremediably lost his footing to the point where he'd become homeless. Then one day he had died. So when I saw François and Diane sitting out there on the pavement, I thought of Mark, this long-forgotten ghost from the past. I hoped that, when he took this long fall, there had been acts of kindness towards him, that there had been outstretched hands on his path, even if he had not been able or willing to seize them.

Mark's picture now sits on my desk. In this picture, this giant of a man tenderly holds a tiny package in his arms—that would be me, forty years ago. That's the only picture I have of Mark, a reminder that we are indeed our brothers' keepers.

GATHAS FOR THE BODHISATTVA WAY

Nathalie, Martine, Serge, Amedeo, Marie-Christine, Marie-Christine, Michel, Pascal

Letting the cat into the house, I vow to meet with gentleness and loving kindness all those who will cross my path—one day at a time.

I vow with all beings to inspire children to seize the present moment and marvel at its beauty.

Meeting my fears as a mental construction without substance, I make the vow to free my mind from everything Prone to pollute the minds of my grandchildren and of all beings.

Watching a leaf fall, Throwing dead leaves onto the compost heap, I vow with all beings to turn my own attachments into fertile soil.

He circles the sky slowly, Focused on finding prey. I will circle the earth slowly, Focused on finding a being I can help.

The tree offers me its bark so I can lean on it. May I with all beings Offer others the refuge Of an undiscriminating compassion.

Gratefully welcoming the flower's smile,

I vow with all beings

To offer my joy to those who cross my path.

One week before passing away, she was helping her son
with his homework.

One hour before passing away, she was writing a text for her
14-year old daughter to read at her funerals.

May I—when the time comes—

Remain a light for others.

CHAPTER FIVE

EIDŌ REINHART

Life is Practice

Living a vowed life has been my intention for most of my adult life, first as a Christian and later as a Buddhist, but my understanding of what that means and what it looks like has changed a lot over the years. Perhaps you, like I, have experienced a conflict between your root tradition and the Buddhist path or between your life and your spiritual practice. I learned eventually that there was no need for conflict and that the Zen path actually helped me to more deeply enter into my root tradition as well as others. It also helped me to embrace my life as my spiritual practice and to live for the benefit of all beings. Eventually I came to understand that no matter where we are or what the circumstances, we are called to a life of vow and repentance and we have the opportunity to live that life right here and right now. Each of us needs to find our own way in our own life. but it's important to realize (and actualize) that any life can be transformed by vow and repentance.

As a young adult I was dissatisfied with life and intuitively felt there must be something more. My search for that "something more" (which I will call "Truth") was my vow. This path or vow led to a quiet inner life and a deeper appreciation of my root tradition, Christianity, and eventually was actualized in zazen.

Initially my question was, "Is there any reason to live?" I experienced a spiritual dimension to life and I wondered if there was any spiritual path which would provide enough meaning or reason to continue living. Could there be some purpose to my life besides just existing? Since I'd been raised as a Christian, my inquiry initially took the form of a number of questions. "Is there a God and does it make any difference?" I'd decided that I didn't have a right or reason to continue living if there was no purpose, so I gave myself a year to figure it out—and this brought up another question: "If I am to continue living, what for?" After pondering it for a year, I realized I couldn't answer it using the intellectual tools on which I had relied so far. My exploration had included a lot of reading in theology and philosophy, including existentialism, yet I couldn't definitively answer "no" to God and realized I never could using my current means. If one can't know about God intellectually, perhaps one could know God directly through one's experience—so, how does one pursue this?

I decided to give my life to this search; this was now my reason to continue living. However, this wasn't just the blind faith of deciding to believe something that couldn't be proven or verified. It was about trying to understand what's meant by God. Who or what is God, and can God be known by one's experience? What are others pointing to when the word "God" is used?

That year of pondering included a lot of quiet time, reflecting on this question, reading and journal writing, and in the process I started developing a very introspective life. I wasn't ready to accept that life was meaningless and had no purpose, and after realizing I couldn't satisfy my curiosity intellectually I was moved toward embracing the question of who God is, rather than whether or not God exists and how I could know him/her/it. I began by searching for a path within the Christian tradition. My reading moved from being primarily intellectual to being more spiritual and inspired. I became acquainted with others who had made a similar choice and by doing so had seemed to have found "something more." Not only did I decide "yes" to God, but I decided to give my life to this pursuit—i.e. finding God, unity with God, knowing God. This was now my vow. I didn't know what this meant, but it became my primary intention and the one that would lead me. It was now the purpose of my life, even if based on a mistaken idea. It was a leap of faith and a profound transformation of my life's intention.

To get there and to continue on this path involved cultivating a habit of interior quiet and doing a lot of spiritual reading, especially about how to pray. I realized I needed quiet time to explore this God, to be with, to know. Thus began a life of prayer, which at this time meant sitting quietly for 30 or more minutes once or twice a day with a receptive heart, letting go of "me" and allowing the light of God to be revealed. For a long time I focused on learning to pray without ceasing as advocated by St Paul. For this I used as a mantra the Jesus Prayer (also known as the Prayer of the Heart). This took several forms: "Lord Jesus Christ, have mercy on me, a sinner"—or "have mercy"—or just "mercy" and eventually just a quiet ascent of intentional love.

Several Biblical passages helped me in my search.
- *Blessed are the pure of heart for they shall see God.* (Matthew 5:8)
- *It is in Him that we live and move and have our being.* (Acts 17:28)
- *Be still and know that I am God.* (Psalm 46:10).
- *The Kingdom of God is within you.* (Luke 17:21)

I was also influenced by other writers, including the anonymous 14th-century author of *The Cloud of Unknowing* who said "Therefore I leave on one side everything I can think, and choose for my love that thing which I cannot think! Why? Because he may well be loved, but not thought. By love he can be caught and held, but by thinking never." We cannot know or experience God by thinking, but only by love. What does it mean to love God?

The Trappist monk Thomas Merton and others remind us that God includes all life, including our own. To love God means to love others as oneself, as we are one body. I am you and you are me. In the New Testament Jesus says that "Whatever you do for the least of these, you do for me." For the Christian, Christ is manifested in everyone as the embodiment of God. You and I are not separate from each other or from God; he is in us and we in him as "It is in Him that we live and move and have our being."

QUIET BEYOND WORDS

I was led to Zen via a long journey in search of the Truth. My initial path via Christianity led me to contemplative prayer, becoming a Roman Catholic, entering a Catholic monastery, and eventually practicing the presence of God in zazen. In the seventies I started exploring Zen and it's Zen that enabled me to continue to be a Christian because Zen helped me to more deeply understand that God/Truth is not separate from me but is in me and I am in "IT." There's no separation. According to Uchiyama Rōshi, "In zazen we can see directly this kingdom within us," and I recognized the truth of this.

As I was seeking God/Truth as a Christian I experienced the yearning expressed in Psalm 43: "As a doe longs for running streams so longs my soul for you, my God. My soul thirsts for God, the God of life: when shall I go to see the face of God? I have no food but tears day and night and all day long men say to me 'Where is your God?' I remember and my soul melts within me; I am on my way to the wonderful Tent, to the house of God, among cries of joy and praise and an exultant throng. Why so downcast, my soul, why do you sigh within me? Put your hope in God: I shall praise him yet, my savior, my God."

I wanted to learn to pray in a way that would lead me to unity with God, to experience God directly. That led to a wordless prayer of surrender which recognized that God was here and now and had never been elsewhere. I understood that the God I was searching for was within me and encompassed me and was actually the cause and source of my search. I just needed to get out of the way to allow God to be revealed. Initially the focus of my spiritual life may have seemed to be primarily about me in that I wanted to experience the "peace beyond understanding," but I also intuitively understood that this "peace" was not just for me but had implications for all beings, as we affect the universe like the ripples of a stone thrown into a pond. I also came to understand that to serve God meant to serve all living beings, as all life included God and was included in God. God was the name some used for this inclusive Reality that could not really be named or understood.

I'd learned from experience that a quiet (non-moving) body helped facilitate interior quiet, but for a long time I didn't have a posture that fostered this. I experimented with various positions including kneeling, as was common in Christian practice, but I didn't succeed in being immobile for more than a few minutes. Eventually my prayer practice led me to Zen, which provided a centuries-old method of being physically still in order to facilitate inner quiet. The Christian tradition provided training in what to do with one's mind and heart, but it didn't provide any instruction in the optimal posture of the body that would help to decrease physical and mental fidgeting. Fortunately,

I discovered zazen in the seventies and it changed my life as I now had a physical method for "practicing the presence of God." Here the point was to let go of my words and thoughts in order to hear God within my heart. The intention of the heart became more important than words; this is where God is revealed and he could be revealed in a heart whose primary intention was love. I came to believe that God did not care about my words, thoughts or beliefs, but instead cared about the intention or purity of the heart.

A favorite Russian story illustrates this beautifully. There were three holy men (*startzi*) who had for decades lived in complete isolation on a small island in the Arctic Sea. A bishop heard of them and decided to pay them a visit. On the shore of the island he found three bearded, toothless old men who bowed low before him. The bishop asked how they prayed and one replied "Ye are three; we are three; have mercy on us." The bishop was amazed at this and began to teach them the "right way" to pray. He taught them the Lord's Prayer until they knew it by heart. They thanked him fervently and the bishop left with a glad heart for performing a good deed. His ship had been sailing for a while when strange clouds formed on the horizon and quickly approached. Suddenly the passengers realized that the clouds were the forms of the *startzi*. The three men bowed low and told the bishop sadly they had forgotten the newly-learnt prayer and asked the bishop to please teach it to them again. Then the bishop crossed himself, bowed to the *startzi* and said: "God will hear your prayer as it is. There is nothing I can teach you. Go and pray for us sinners." The bishop prostrated himself before them and they turned around and went over the water back to the island. Until dawn, a light streamed forth at the place where the pious *startzi* had vanished.

The bishop learned from this encounter that these *startzi* were very close to God even without using the "correct" words in their prayer. On encountering them, he'd concluded that not only were they using the "wrong" words, but their prayer was nonsensical. He tried to teach them the "right" way to pray and discovered that these men were already in communion with God, as evidenced by their holy lives and miraculous appearance across the water. God apparently didn't need the correct words but responded instead to the love and purity of heart manifested by these holy men.

TO WILL ONE THING

The understanding of my vow continued to evolve, and through the Christian portion of this journey, I began to focus on the Christian existentialist Søren Kierkegaard's phrase "Purity of heart is to will [intend] one thing." My intention was now to cultivate purity of heart and to will one thing—the "one thing" could be understood as God's will, as in "not as I will, but as you will." (Matthew 26:39). To have this intention meant to be continually letting go of my own will or ego and allowing God to act and speak through me. This meant, among other things, to live each moment wholeheartedly, giving myself completely to this moment. To "will one thing," one must be continually discerning what God's will is in this moment. What's this moment asking of me? To know this requires inner quiet in order to allow the heart, or God, to inform me. It's not enough to do God's will—one's will must become God's. I also understood "willing one thing" to mean wholeheartedly intending what's in each moment, whether that's washing the dishes or mowing the lawn, acting with purity of heart and purity of intention, not with heart and mind divided or wanting to be elsewhere. This is to act with love. God can only be found in the here-and-now of this moment, so to find "IT" in this moment or this activity requires giving oneself 100% to what is. Everything is for the glory and love of God, no matter how big or small; everything is to be done with intention and with one mind and one heart.

Can one will (intend) only one thing—and if so, what is that one thing? Truth? God? God's will? Salvation? Salvation for me? Or for all beings? It could not be salvation, as that would be seeking a reward or having a goal, the goal being to get something from God—to achieve something, to reach something. No, to live with purity of heart and to "will one thing" meant that the one thing could only be God (Truth/Love)—that is, all intention and action is for love of God, and that translates into love of all beings. Yet this is still speaking of God as a reality that's at least partially separate from myself. This is almost inevitable when one uses a word for "IT," because naming it makes it an object of this subject.

My prayer became a wordless surrender of the heart to love, with the conviction and faith that my will or ego could be replaced by the will of God, if I let go of my self and let God take over. I had to want what God wants. I also trusted that this existential posture of the heart had the power to transform the self as well as the entire universe. Why? Because I'm not a separate entity from the universe (Reality/God); I am the universe and the universe is me, so if I'm saved, then the universe is saved.

This conviction was enough to motivate me to sit in silence and listen to my heart, which was also the heart of the universe or God's heart. I now understood that one couldn't know anything about God with the intellect but perhaps could "know" God from experience by being quiet and listening, by penetrating deeply within one's heart and loving...and that this knowing and loving had the potential to transform the universe. This "God" was perhaps another name for Reality or "the ground of being" as described by theologian Paul Tillich or by Buddhists as Thusness or Suchness. I stopped using a name because to name it immediately placed "it" outside of myself.

My interior life became quieter and quieter and I sat in zazen with no expectation, as to have a goal would be dualistic and that would not be "willing one thing." How can I "will one thing" if what I'm doing is just a means to an end? That isn't one thing, it's two things: the doing (means) and the reward (end). The doing (practice) is not the means, it's the "end." It's the actualization. As a Christian, I realized that to want something from God, even my own salvation or healing of others, wasn't embracing God with one mind and one heart —it wasn't wanting or loving God for his own sake. To want something as a reward or consequence, even if it's a good thing, was still not on the mark. It was doing or willing for something else, something other than the thing itself. In Christian terms, this could be stated as "doing all for the glory [love] of God," not for some benefit. Although there could be consequences, even good ones, to practice or pray with a goal wasn't the practice for the "pure of heart;" it wasn't "willing one thing." But even "doing all for the glory [love] of God" implies there is a God separate from me.

DISCOVERING ZEN

There were two statements by Zen masters that had a great impact on me. Jōshu Sasaki Rōshi said, "There is no God but he is always with you," and Eihei Dōgen said "Practice and realization are one." Practice is not a means to get enlightenment; it's the end. It is enlightenment itself. What we're seeking is already here, and we just need to get out of the way so we can be aware of IT and be IT. "The kingdom of God is within." We need to seek the light that's within us. The Truth is paradoxical.

This was my understanding at the time I discovered Zen practice. Zazen and prayer had been means to unity with God but now were the practice of the presence of God— but even saying the "presence" makes it sound like we're speaking of another entity. Perhaps it could be better said that zazen was the realization, manifestation, and actualization of the presence of God, or the actualization of God or of love. Eventually the naming of "IT" became not only unhelpful, but an obstacle.

Recently I recalled that in the seventies when I was discovering Zen, and before I entered the Catholic monastery, I had already read Kōshō Uchiyama's book *Approach to Zen*, written in 1973. I'm sure it contributed to my spiritual formation, even though I may not have realized the significance of it at the time. When I entered the Poor Clare monastery in 1979, I was already practicing daily zazen and I took Uchiyama's book with me and added it to the monastery library. When I left in 1980, I took the book back out with me and still have it. I appreciated Uchiyama's understanding of Westerners and his explanations made sense to me. He even quoted the Bible, which was helpful to me as a Christian, as I felt understood by him and vice versa. He spoke my language.

This was over a decade before I met Okumura Rōshi in the early nineties when he was interim teacher at Minnesota Zen Meditation Center. By the time I met Okumura Rōshi, I was married and had two young sons, so life was quite full with my domestic responsibilities and professional life as a physical therapist. I had always had a yearning for monastic life, but now I was a householder and, to be honest, I didn't value domestic life as much as I did the religious life. Embracing this life was a struggle for me, as I often felt there was a conflict between my actual life and the life of practice I thought I should be living.

I continued on parallel paths with Christianity and Buddhism for quite some time and I received the precepts from Okumura Rōshi in the nineties. By this time he was no longer in Minneapolis, where I lived, and thus started a long-distance student-teacher relationship.

ACTUAL LIFE AS SPIRITUAL LIFE

Eventually I was ordained and received transmission, and in some ways, my conflicts escalated. Now I felt even more obligation to "practice" and wasn't yet able to see that my life was practice. I was still looking forward to a time when my life wouldn't be divided, not realizing that the division was within me and totally unnecessary. I hadn't yet been able to embrace my life as practice and practice as life, and I compared myself to others. People often asked me, "What are you going to do now?" especially after I received transmission. There seemed to be an expectation that I wasn't meeting, and I felt something was lacking. I would occasionally consult with Okumura Rōshi, who was not very directive but his few words were usually wise. Once when I was agonizing over this conflict, he said, "Your sangha is whoever needs you most, and right now that's your family and your patients." What a relief and revelation that was! I knew this but hadn't been able to embrace it, and his words helped me to begin to embrace my life. Still, it took a long time before I actually experienced my life as practice.

I'm reminded of a story I heard once about a conversation between two practitioners. One said she was annoyed when Zen students who are parents use their family as an excuse not to practice, and the other said it was even more annoying when such students use their practice as an excuse not to parent. I think I had been at risk of living this confusing dichotomy.

In the early nineties when Okumura Rōshi was the interim teacher at MZMC, I had been practicing for about 15 years a zazen without expectation, but I hadn't done much studying, so I didn't actually know much about Buddhism. What I knew about was zazen and its transforming power. I didn't value study and, in fact, had some reservations about its value because of my previous disillusionment with intellectual pursuit of a spiritual path. I had become skeptical and even fearful that study might too easily lead my mind away from my heart by filling my mind with ideas and concepts that, instead of being helpful, might actually be a hindrance to practice. However, I observed and learned from Okumura Rōshi, who embodied a peaceful, upright bearing as well as a commitment to study. I started learning more about Buddhism and gradually embraced the teachings more and more. I found that instead of interfering with practice, this understanding nourished it. I was especially drawn to the core teachings, including the bodhisattva vows and the understanding of vow and repentance.

UNATTAINABLE VOWS

The most important aspect of these vows and what makes them so beautiful is that they are unattainable. They give us a direction, but not a goal we can achieve. We're never done with these intentions, these vows; they're perpetual and eternal and provide the grounds for ongoing repentance. Uchiyama Rōshi said, "In our zazen, precisely since we have taken such a vow, we cannot help but depend on being unable to fulfill it." Because we can't actually do it no matter how hard we try, we need to continually return to the intention of our vows, make repentance, and give ourselves again and again to living with these intentions. If we had vows we could achieve, then these would be our goals—and if and when we reach them, then what? Are we done? No, this work is never done, and thus we must continually renew these vows and repent. This repentance isn't about saying "I'm sorry" or feeling regret. It's a complete turning around, standing up and starting again to live these vows wholeheartedly, regardless of whether or not they're attainable. If I help to free one person, is that enough? No. How about 10? How about 1000? And would we even know if we had helped to free someone? No. We need to give ourselves to these intentions wholeheartedly without any thought or measurement of success, for we cannot know the consequences of our actions; we can only intend with purity of heart and continually repent and renew our vows.

The bodhisatva vows are also expressed in the Three Pure Precepts:

> *With purity of heart, I vow to abstain from all action*
> *that creates harm.*
> *With purity of heart, I vow to make every effort to do*
> *all that is wholesome.*
> *With purity of heart, I vow to benefit all beings.*

These three vows are also stated in various other ways:

> *I vow to avoid all evil, to practice good, and to save/free*
> *all sentient beings.*

> *I vow to avoid all action that creates clinging,*
> *to do all that is good, and to live for the benefit*
> *of all beings.*

In my mind, this last sentence sums up all vows; our vow is to live for the benefit of all beings; i.e. to live with the intention of compassion for all beings. This is purity of heart; this is "willing one thing." We're willing—intending with every thought and action—the benefit of all beings. A question for us is: How can I do this within the context of the life I have been given?

WHAT IS PRACTICE?

This brings us to the question of what qualifies as practice. This has been an ongoing question in my life, as I struggled for years *believing* my life was practice but not *experiencing* this. However, practice is our lives, whatever our lives are. Our lives are our arena for practice; it's the place where we live our vows; it's the situation that provides us with the opportunity to live in vow. If it can't be in our lives as they are, it can't be anywhere. We need to look at our lives and discern how to live our vow here and now in these circumstances.

I'd always thought the ideal place was a monastery, and anything else was not as good or as possible. Certainly the monastic life gives us some opportunities that householder life doesn't, but it may not be as ideal as we might expect, partly because we bring ourselves and our lives with us to the monastery or wherever we live. Being human and imperfect, we face many of the same dilemmas and challenges as we would anywhere. Another way to think about this is that to live in an ideal environment that's conducive to practice might make some things easier, but householder life provides many other opportunities and challenges not available in the monastery. For example, to live simply is easier in the monastery because it's already set up for this type of life. Therefore, one doesn't need to make constant decisions about every detail of life; the context is provided in a monastery. But in the world, a simple life is constantly challenged by our circumstances. If we're parents, we need to provide food and shelter and maybe college tuition for our children. Can we live in this affluent culture and not be attached to material things? These challenges can help keep us aware, alert, and mindful because these are ongoing questions to be discerned in light of our vows.

One of the problems I had after leaving the Christian monastery was that I felt guilty for having or enjoying things, and therefore I felt guilty much of the time, instead of grateful. I struggled with this for a long time. Guilt is not a good motivator or healthy mindset. I eventually learned to appreciate and enjoy the myriad things life had to offer, including colors, hats, warmth, family, work—in short, to be grateful for the opportunity of this life, a precious opportunity indeed. We have so much to be grateful for; there's no need for guilt. To determine one's level of detachment, one can just picture a highly valued item and consider how it would feel to give it away. If you can give it away, you are not attached to it, but in the meantime while you have it, can you enjoy, appreciate, and be grateful for it as opposed to feeling guilty for having it?

If we live in the world we usually need to make a living somehow. I have been doing that as a physical therapist for more than 45 years, and for decades I saw this only as a means to an end and looked forward to a time when I no longer had to work, so I could devote more time to "practice." Now I've reached the age of retirement but I'm still working. Why? Because when I finally embraced my livelihood as my practice, my work life was completely transformed. I could give myself to it wholeheartedly without reservation, without conflict, without thinking I should be elsewhere. That's a transforming realization. Why do I continue to work as a PT? Because I am a PT and this is my way of serving. This is my practice and it's a big part of how I can live for the benefit of others. I need not be doing something else in some other place. It need not be recognizable as a religious or spiritual practice, but it is if I am living in vow. This can be done in any place or circumstance. and living our lives as wholehearted practice is what our vows ask of us.

Uchiyama Rōshi said, "There is no purer way of expressing this attitude toward prayer than zazen…The essence of this pure prayer is all included in the prayer that takes the form of zazen. How can we approach truth—or to a Christian, God—through the zazen we practice with bodies that are full of confusion and evil? For that zazen must have vow and repentance as a backing. To express this from the opposite side, zazen as true religion must include vow and repentance. Doing zazen is throwing out all human thought and this letting go constitutes the throwing out of man's arrogance. In doing so, we become, as the Bible says, 'as God wills,' and then 'the works of God will be manifest (John 9:3).'"

In Okumura Rōshi's commentary on the *Heart Sutra* he says, "When we see emptiness, we realize there's no hindrance, no obstacles to block our life force. It is soft and flexible, like a plant that tries to go around a big rock and continues to grow. There is always some other way to live, to grow."

Thus my hope for us all is that we'll see the road we're on and embrace it, give ourselves to it with one heart and mind, and be grateful for the amazing opportunity given to us by this life to live the vow to benefit all beings. This means living a life of compassion for all.

CHAPTER SIX

DŌJU LAYTON

My Absurd Vow

I became a priest less than a year ago. Perhaps because of this, it has been difficult for me to quickly define a vow for the rest of my life of practice. More likely, however, I am simply finding the basic Buddhist vows—not to mention the expectations of intensive zazen practice in my particular lineage—burdensome enough. Of course, given the nature of the vows we take, I think this must be the case for any Buddhist. Beginning with the bodhisattva vows, we vow to help all beings awaken to true reality, to end all of our delusions, to learn everything there is to know about the dharma, and to follow the Buddha way to its conclusion. Not only are these exceptionally difficult things to try to do, they are also logically absurd. They simply cannot be completed, even if we really had a series of lifetimes in which to try. The pure precepts add that we must fully embrace the moral codes of our society and community, and only act in a way that is beneficial. Finally, among the ten major precepts, we vow not to become angry and not to criticize others, two rather basic human tendencies. Although none of these are absolute commandments and none are expected to be observed perfectly, they are nonetheless daunting oaths to make. So can I really add a personal vow on top of this? Perhaps it would make sense to explore the nature of these basic vows before getting too far ahead of ourselves.

On a number of occasions, the heavy burden of my vows has led me to think of the ancient Greek myth of Sisyphus. We are told that Sisyphus was a king famed for his craftiness. Among other things, he stole secrets known only to the gods and escaped from the realm of the dead on two separate occasions. Because he was able to out-smart the gods repeatedly, he began to think himself equal to them. Being a mortal human, however, in the end he met his inevitable fate and was dragged to the underworld for good. In punishment for his life of trickery, Zeus decided to have him carry a boulder up a long, steep hill. The rock was enchanted so that it would always roll back down to the bottom of the hill whenever Sisyphus neared the top. He would then have to walk back down, start over again, and repeat the dull procedure for all eternity.

In becoming Buddhists, we see the emptiness of our usual lives of trickery and self-enrichment and we willingly aim to give them up. We take on the cosmically heavy task of helping to bring a healthy way of life to all beings in the universe (including ourselves, of course), which is quite like carrying a massive boulder uphill. But because we are humans with all of our deep flaws, we are inevitably bound to fail, and fail often. As soon as we might think we are doing a great job, it does not take long for the boulder to roll back down the hill, forcing us to start all over. This act of picking up the rock once again is analogous to Buddhist repentance, the acknowledgment to ourselves that we have fallen short of our aims and the restatement of our commitment to continue carrying them out. This practice of repentance must work in tandem with our vows for them to be worth taking. Because as humans we fail so often, we have to be able to see our shortcomings and renew our pledge to follow the Way. However, the ancient Greek myth clearly does not form a perfect analogy with our practice, because we as Buddhists willingly take on our vows; they are not a punishment from up on high, but a commitment made from our own depths to understand ourselves, to make the world a place worth living in, even if it requires Herculean effort beyond what we think possible.

Perhaps, however, there is a way out of this Sisyphean approach to practice. In Dōgen's conception of Buddhism, we read that all of the precepts are completely actualized in our zazen practice. While sitting facing the wall, we can do no wrong. In the interconnection in which we find ourselves, all beings are freed, delusions disappear, the Dharma is mastered, and the Buddha way is complete. In other words, this is the only place where we find our vows fulfilled. Extending our Sisyphean metaphor to zazen, the boulder is already at the top of the hill, or perhaps it would be more appropriate to say that the boulder, the hill, and Sisyphus all just disappear. While I believe all of this to be true, practically speaking we cannot hope to have the benefit of this putative loophole unless we actually sit down and really practice zazen. We may be dwelling constantly in interconnection, but unless we see it and embrace it, our lives remain the same as ever. This, unfortunately, calls into question just how much of a loophole it really is. Zazen does not just happen of its own accord. We have to vow to do zazen with regularity, despite whatever else might be pulling us to do something else more interesting, more exciting, or seemingly more important. For me, this unspoken vow is the hardest of all.

I find this vow so difficult because I have lived my whole life intensely focused on one thing for some period of time, only to abandon it for the next thing that strikes my fancy. I can be exceptionally driven, but usually only when my interest is fully piqued. Zazen did this for quite some time, but staring at a wall can only keep you excited for so long. In *Shōbōgenzō Zuimonki*, Dōgen must mention a hundred times that to practice Zen one must have single-minded focus and throw away all other pursuits. For me, that's a more foreign concept than any of the Buddhist practices that I initially found so unfamiliar. Somehow, even though zazen no longer exactly gets me excited, I know that it is like medicine to me, so I keep doing it. Nonetheless, I often feel more like Sisyphus than I did early in my practice. The Dharma somehow compels me to carry the rock up the hill, but I struggle.

I think that this must be a somewhat common problem, however. Although I might represent the negative end of the single-mindedness spectrum, the traditional Buddhist system of monasticism seems to exist in large part to help monks keep each other motivated precisely because it is so easy to stray from the path. After all, very few people have the single-mindedness to do what the Buddha is said to have done and sit zazen alone under a tree for days on end with no encouragement from anyone. Therefore, part of my difficulty in following this vow of zazen stems not so much from the zazen itself—although it is not especially easy at times—but rather it is due to the fact that our temple, Sanshinji, is something halfway between a typical American Zen center and a traditional live-in monastery. Zen centers tend to usually operate somewhat like a local church, with parishioners visiting at set times during the week but virtually never holding events as intensive as our five-day sesshins, in which we do zazen for fourteen hours each day. In a monastery, practice takes place twenty-four hours a day like the tides of an ocean: whatever one's wishes might be, one can't escape their force and has no choice but to rise and fall along with them. In such a place, one's tendencies to go in other directions are kept in check.

In the case of Sanshinji, all of my teacher's students-in-training live in their own homes and must support their own lives. In this situation, the tidal force at work is that of normal secular life, and getting to Sanshinji to practice requires fighting against it. The karma of my entire life pulls me towards doing all of the various things that I have been accustomed to doing since long before I knew what Zen was. There is no good system in place, other than my own will, to prevent distractions, and my own will is usually not an especially good system. As if that were not enough, my teacher is the precise opposite of a micro-manager. He does not provide voluntary critiques of an individual's practice (though he will if we take the initiative to ask). Unfortunately, I cannot complain because he makes it perfectly clear to the students he takes on that he will not babysit them in their practice. When he is asked to ordain a student, he explains that he will have his own eyes on Buddha, and the student must as well. As a result, our practice is completely up to us. Unlike at a monastery, if we do not feel like practicing, no one will tell us we are doing anything wrong. Because, as I've noted, my motivation tends to be so fickle, I have found it difficult to keep my own eyes on Buddha. Ultimately, though, it is the only way things can be, because our practice can only exist independently with our own personal commitment. If one's practice is completely dependent on a monastery, then it might be hard to call that a truly sincere practice. That being said, I am coming to find that Buddhism exists at the intersection of self-improvement and self-acceptance. I might not ever be able to improve my discipline to the level of my teacher or my other dharma ancestors, but I am finding that as long as I stick with my practice, however many times I might drop the rock climbing up the hill, that is enough.

Again, the major difference between Sisyphus and us is that he had no say in his fate, whereas we bear the boulder of our own free will. Unlike Sisyphus, we can leave the rock at the bottom of the hill, go home, and never come back to carry it again. In fact, this raises a fundamental question that has not yet been directly addressed. Why do we bother with our vows? If we know they cannot be accomplished in a lifetime or more, our practice is supposed to be about removing the suffering in our lives, and zazen cannot compare with Netflix for entertainment value, why should we follow such a frustrating path? Again, Sisyphus provides an answer, this time via Albert Camus, the 20th-century French philosopher, but to arrive at that answer will take a bit of explanation. Camus is remembered for his writings on "the Absurd," which he described as the unending human desire for meaning, when it is in fact always out of human reach. In his essay *The Myth of Sisyphus*, he asks a morbid question: does becoming conscious of this purported impossibility of attaining meaning suggest that we should kill ourselves? His conclusion is that to kill oneself actually increases the meaninglessness of one's life; to do so would make it even more absurd. Ignoring the problem, once aware of it, likewise increases the absurdity of our position. According to Camus, we should instead not only embrace the paradox of seeking meaning that we cannot hold onto, but further we should continue to seek meaning in the full awareness of its futility. Fittingly, he describes Sisyphus as "the absurd hero" because of his eternal fate to carry out a futile task.

This all might seem very depressing at face value, though actually the opposite is the case, but we have to understand what is meant by "meaning" and how Buddhism relates to it. Unlike the European tradition, "meaning" per se is not something Buddhism seeks. Meaning is usually conceived of as something essential and unchanging (if we could only find it), which is precisely the kind of thing that Buddhism rejects as an ultimate source of our suffering. What we seek is harmony with the present, harmony with others, and harmony with ourselves. Because the present, the people around us, and ourselves are always changing, harmony with these things does not violate the Buddhist principle of impermanence. We can call this "meaning," but if it is, it is important to see that it is not this frozen, unchanging kind of meaning that Camus also rejected. Indeed, D.T. Suzuki defined it in these terms when he said that we do not need to ask where we can find meaning, but rather we must see that life itself is meaning. However we define it, what we seek is to really live life itself and not just the life of the small, limited self. However, we still have to take a vow to see life this way; it does not happen without great effort. I think this is essentially what Camus meant by concluding that we should embrace the impossibility of finding meaning while still striving for it. It is not that life is meaningless, in the way that we would usually interpret such a notion, but rather that "meaning" is just another idea that separates us from actual reality. Really, it is in the dynamic process of seeking where something like meaning appears, not as something we might attain and hold onto. Camus' "There is no such thing as meaning, but that's okay" is functionally the same as Suzuki's "Life itself is meaning"; in the same manner we use the Buddhist terms "emptiness" and "interconnection" to mean the same ultimately positive thing. If you are obsessed with finding meaning, it might be more helpful to follow Camus' logic so that you can let go of that conceptual way of thinking. If you really think life is meaningless (in the depressed sense), Suzuki's more positive statement is likely more helpful. The point is that Camus is not making an argument to justify sadness, but that he is really aiming at something life-affirming.

Getting back to our question: why, then, should we stick to our vows when we could do any number of other more pleasurable things? For me, the reason is the same as my reason for coming to Buddhism in the first place. Often, we take up this practice because we examine the way humans usually live and see that it is devoid of meaning, or at least what we think meaning should be. People live brief lives in which they aim to satisfy their small desires and then die. Some may seek solace in an abstract belief in a transcendent realm, but most who become Buddhists in the West find this to be an unreliable source of this thing we call meaning. It is this consciousness of the meaninglessness of normal human life that drives us to this practice. Likewise, even if we begin to see our vows as futile or overly burdensome, if the alternative to keeping them is returning to the meaninglessness of the normal human position, we have little choice but to continue on our path. In fact, in the Buddhist tradition it is said that once we take our vows, they can never be undone. When I first heard this, I thought it was just fancy rhetoric, but having tried several times to talk myself into doing something else with my life, I have found that to do so would require willful ignorance of why I wanted to become a Buddhist to begin with. Once sincere faith in Buddhist principles has arisen, difficulty is not enough to make us abandon them. Our unfulfillable vows, then, are our embrace of the Absurd; we know they cannot be achieved, but we must willingly continue to aim at them regardless. It is only on such a path that something we might call meaning arises.

The bodhisattva vows are both a complete acknowledgement of what Camus would call our absurd human position and the ultimate realm of dynamic meaning. To understand why this is the case, we need to look briefly at the development of Buddhism. For the pre-Buddhist Indian, samsara—the cycle of birth and death—was the source of perceived meaninglessness in life: we must pointlessly transmigrate from one life to the next, doomed to always suffer again even if we might rid ourselves of it temporarily. Buddhism added an escape from meaninglessness via the attainment of nirvana, resulting in being released from samsara at death. The belief at that time was that once so-called enlightenment was attained, one would no longer be reborn after death. Thus in the early Buddhist tradition we could say that nirvana was meaning and samsara meaninglessness. However, as Buddhism developed, the understanding of nirvana changed dramatically. Several centuries after the death of the Buddha, nirvana came to be seen not as an escape from samsara, but a radical acceptance of it. This is why Nagarjuna wrote "There is not the slightest distinction between samsara and nirvana." And yet, the early analysis that samsara is meaninglessness and nirvana is meaning in a sense still holds. For Nagarjuna and the millions of Mahayana Buddhists after him, we could say that meaning must be found in meaninglessness. However, because the bodhisattva does not allow herself to attain nirvana while others still seek it, like Camus, meaning-as-nirvana is out of grasp. The bodhisattva vows, in explicitly stating that they are too vast to be achieved despite our vow to carry them out, parallel Camus' idea that meaning can never be obtained, and yet we must seek it anyway. Again, we must not see this as negative. Camus and Dōgen tell us why.

In *The Myth of Sisyphus*, Camus writes that, "Happiness and the absurd are two sons of the same earth. They are inseparable." He means that we only find true happiness when we are fully aware and accepting of the absurd human condition that drives us to seek meaning yet never find it. Normally we would think that we must first find meaning, and then as a result we will be happy, but Camus rejects this idea. Dōgen's claim that "practice and enlightenment are one" is virtually the same. When Dōgen wrote this famous saying, the first half was paraphrased from a common description of the

115

Buddhist path: hear, think, practice, enlightenment. Traditionally, the Buddhist path was perceived as a series of steps, starting with hearing about Buddhist ideas and ending with enlightenment. Dōgen tells us that the sincere carrying out of this path is itself enlightenment. Camus concludes his essay on Sisyphus by writing, "The struggle itself toward the heights is enough to fill a man's heart. One must imagine Sisyphus happy." In other words, the path is where we find contentment, or, though Camus would object to the word choice, it is where we find meaning. The path is nothing other than our vows. Therefore, our vows can be the only source of happiness, enlightenment, or even what we might call meaning.

Normally, Zen is seen as a difficult practice that few would be willing to undertake. I do not think that this view is necessarily incorrect, but for me it is a difficult practice that I cannot help but to undertake despite the fact that I may not be especially well-suited to it. Just as Sisyphus, proud and devious, was by design not the appropriate person to carry out his task from which there was no escape and no glory, I similarly lack the single-mindedness that Dōgen praises so highly in Zen practice. Nonetheless, like Camus' version of Sisyphus, here is where I must stand in defiance of my karma and state the only personal vow I can think to make. I vow to keep practicing despite whatever current might be flowing against me. I vow to take up the burden of the rock when it rolls back down the hill, regardless of how long I might drag my feet on the way back down. I vow to keep showing up to the zendo even if I sleep through a full week of early-morning zazen. I vow to find serenity within the realm of human failure. I vow to continue to embrace our absurd practice, because to do otherwise is the only thing that would be more absurd.

Completely Receiving, Completely Releasing

Considering what to write for this book has been interesting. As I reflected on my own path and practice of vow, I began to consider just when it was I started my own investigation into precisely what my individual vow would be. The more I considered it, the more I saw there's no clearly identifiable moment in which my search or investigation began. I believe that is because what we call the bodhisattva vow in Mahayana Buddhism is fundamentally what might more commonly be called the instinct or drive of a human life to become fully mature, to become an adult. So to my mind, we begin this process of realizing our vow at the moment of birth.

In my case, then, I could begin the narrative describing the unfolding of my vow on December 3, 1961, the day I was born. But I don't think that would be particularly interesting to readers or to myself, so I'll pick a later time that seems to specifically illustrate, perhaps, some circumstances that have nurtured and encouraged this expression of the bodhisattva vow as a function of my own life.

Perhaps November of 2003 is as good a place as any to start. I had traveled to Bloomington, Indiana, to participate in the first *genzo-e* retreat my teacher offered at his new temple, Sanshinji. At that time, I definitely realized I was desperately searching for something. I was shouldering during that retreat some of the most intense and difficult suffering I had ever experienced. It had taken root as a result of some difficulties I had encountered in some intimate interpersonal relationships. I felt emotionally raw and vulnerable, but at the same time I felt the pain had somehow opened my heart and brought to the forefront of my life its most fundamental and important questions. Some of those questions included, " Who am I, really?" "What is the value of my life?" and "What will be my contribution in this life?"

It was in this painful yet open emotional state that I returned to Bloomington a couple of months later in January of 2004 to create a new life for myself and study the dharma. At that time I basically felt I no longer knew who I was. I also wondered how I would support myself financially and what my role at the new temple would be.

It had been Okumura Rōshi's ability to communicate and embody his understanding of zazen practice as dharma that had drawn me there. I had encountered something truly unique and profound, and I was determined to stay in Bloomington and practice and study as best I could. Amidst all the pain and grief, I somehow knew I had found the direction in which I needed to proceed. I had found my true teacher and I had encountered the style of practice in which my life could blossom.

So I did what I needed to do to continue to live and practice in Bloomington. At first I had very little rent money, so I lived with sangha members, new friends, and I even bunked in Sanshinji's new zendo for the better part of a year. It was also difficult to find work at first, since I was determined to attend all of Sanshinji's practice events, including a monthly retreat/sesshin. But I'm very grateful that soon after arriving in Bloomington, Hosshin Michael Shoaf regularly offered me work assisting him with his home remodeling business, and many other people also supported me in many different ways. I'm so grateful for the financial help, encouragement, and kindness I received during the time I lived in Bloomington from January 2003 to January 2009.

During this time Sanshinji was a brand new temple, and those of us who had arrived there to practice with Okumura Rōshi and his community had a sense we were helping to establish a truly unique practice situation. As I began to settle, soaking in the amazing teachings I encountered, embracing zazen practice, and doing what I could to make a contribution to the community, the emphasis on living by vow in Uchiyama Rōshi's and Okumura Rōshi's teachings and practice became clearer. I tried mainly to focus on what I was doing at Sanshinji as the expression of my vow, but more and more the question arose of how I would continue to express this vow in my own unique way after my five-year training period at Sanshinji had been completed.

The period immediately following my arrival in Bloomington I spent fretting somewhat over the increasingly obvious truth that I would never probe the depths of Dōgen Zenji's writings, in the original ancient Chinese and Japanese, that my teacher had. Considering I was already in my early 40s and it takes most people ten years to learn enough kanji simply to read a modern Japanese news story, I clearly saw I wouldn't be able to follow in my teacher's footsteps in this regard.

Yet I was comforted by Uchiyama Rōshi's words, "A rose blossoms as a rose, and a violet blossoms as a violet." So as the weeks, months and years passed, I continued to consider the question of discovering my own unique expression of vow. Eventually I came to understand that this discovery would arrive of its own accord if I continued to settle into my practice, into deeply facing my life.

Part of this settling process entailed doing seven sesshins and three community retreats per year. The sesshins, especially at the beginning, were very difficult both physically and emotionally. Uchiyama Rōshi of course called them "sesshins without toys," and they consisted almost entirely of zazen practice from 4 am to 9 pm for five or seven days. At first these sesshins seemed to me a sort of premeditated monthly crisis. However, I eventually came to feel they were my ultimate refuge and most profound teacher, and I began to understand that the depth of Okumura Rōshi's teachings was inseparably connected to his years of practicing in this way.

So at last it occurred to me I could possibly help others to encounter this style of "no toys"sesshin some day. As far as I knew, there was only one other place in North America, Pioneer Valley Zendo in Massachusetts, that offered this sesshin on a monthly basis. Perhaps, as the realization of my particular bodhisattva vow, I could somehow help establish a place centered on practicing in this way.

Incredibly, by July of 2011, with the help of many people—most notably that of one very kind and generous benefactor—a piece of land with a cabin was purchased in the Ozark Mountains of northwest Arkansas. I named the small practice place Gyōbutsuji, after Dōgen Zenji's *Shōbōgenzō Gyōbutsu Igi* (Dignified Conduct of Practice Buddha). Gyōbutsuji is dedicated to offering the sesshin practice I inherited in Bloomington.

When considering what I would write for this book, I knew my challenge would be in communicating the depth of impact this sesshin has had on my life. It has "saved" me, to again use the words of Uchiyama Rōshi; it has given my life direction and provided it with a solid foundation for practice and reflection.

Then at some point it occurred to me I could use the "sesshin journal" I have been keeping since 2008 to illustrate some of the influence this practice has had on my life. The rest of this chapter is composed of excerpts from that journal.

The excerpts represent only a fraction of the entries I made over the years, and the entries that do appear are only partial. I chose from some of the excerpts I thought represented a few of the concrete, experiential teachings I had received from sesshin. I tried not to edit them too heavily, thought I did cut out most of the proper names and I added a sentence or two here and there for clarification.

At this point I would like to thank my teacher for introducing me to this style of sesshin practice and for explaining to me, and so many others, its meaning within the context of Dōgen Zenji's teachings and Buddhism in general. I am forever in his debt for his willingness to accept me into his sangha at a very difficult time in my life and for showing me through his practice example and teachings that zazen really is my most venerable and true teacher.

I sincerely hope readers find the following excerpts interesting and in some way inspiring. As I read over them again myself, I couldn't help but think so much is missing. My attempts to communicate the "value" of this invaluable practice just seem to fall so very short. Nonetheless, here they are.

2008
FEBRUARY SESSHIN, SANSHINJI

...I'm having that typical "cleansed" feeling today, recognizing the elementary connection with life again. How do I lose track of it even though it is so familiar at these times? I guess thinking just takes over eventually; so many conceptual concerns to pull me away from this simplicity, I suppose. Sesshin is the only time it is so clear that thinking is truly a minor part of life. What a relief! It allows me to come back to myself, back to life, back to simplicity. Isn't this faith itself? Isn't the simple joy in feeling my heart beat, hearing my robes rustle, and listening to the wind, the awakening to compassion? Sesshin is vital to my health it seems, though I don't always enjoy it. Its beautiful and wondrous faith returns by doing nothing....

.... [A change of subject, later in the same entry] More clarity these post-sesshin days about the relationship between suffering, time and self... Basically, all suffering is a function of these two things. In my case, this suffering often manifests as frustration or anxiety about not getting enough done during the day or having too many things to do. I can really see that the root of this suffering is the fight against time: trying to beat time or trying to make time conform to my idea of productivity or relaxation. So this is clinging to the self's agenda, clinging to the self itself, actually. Self is being reified in the resistance to time. But to end suffering is to end this battle with time, and I think this is what happens in sesshin. In sesshin sooner or later I have to give up trying to push through the slow, tedious, passage of time. Eventually I have to just become completely one with time, sink into it fully; this means time dissolves, or perhaps we can say I dissolve into time. I have to surrender to time, and this means surrendering the self, surrendering to self, even? This is not mystical or mysterious, it is simply being present, of course, but "being present" seems to imply some skill or facility on the part of the one "doing the being." But this isn't what happens in sesshin. I think the mind instead finally just tires of the fight and simply lets time be what it is, lets the self be what it is. There is nothing heroic or skillful about it. The conditions of sesshin itself (which do include me and all of my delusion) are what create this dissolving into time. I think of this as "non-doing" (無為 *mu-i*). It is giving up the goal but still "doing" for the sake of doing, surrendering the self to doing and becoming one with time. There is still holding the posture in zazen, for example, but I can never really know if "I am hitting the mark" of the "right posture" or if "I" am ever really "doing zazen" (or if zazen is ever really "doing me"), because hitting the mark involves completely letting go of knowing. Hitting the mark is opening the hand, and the mark itself is perhaps a product of the hand's grasping....

Yet because of this, there is relief and infinite freedom within sesshin: there is no more wondering about the next thing to do, no more fretting over whether I've accomplished enough or even if I'm performing well enough. I think "non-doing" can happen in any other activity such as playing music, cooking, or taking a pee, but in sesshin a special set of conditions are created to support non-doing...

JUNE SESSHIN, VIRGINIA

...I think most people of "Western" culture have so much self-disdain and self-hatred, and we look to improve our "self-esteem" to remedy this. Usually we don't want to receive ourselves in this moment, we want to push it away until we can fix it, make it what we think it should be... But simple self-esteem can never hold up, it seems to me, to all life shows us about ourselves, if we really see who we are. We all have dark aspects of ourselves. I think I will always find something about myself I can dislike on a conventional level. That's not so much of a problem, really, since self-reflection helps me to improve. But there is a tendency to reify the negative qualities and so reify self. The only way to avoid this kind of reification and ultimately accept this "me" is to let go of self-judgments, along with all other mental/emotional experience. That is zazen. Yet when the dark things do come up, they must be received. They can't be released until they are completely received. That receiving is also zazen. Trying to avoid them is no different than clinging to them.

When we shun something about ourselves, reject it, or hide it away, we are actually reifying it, strangely enough. This is the same as self-despising; by rejecting ourselves we are actually clinging to ourselves. I suppose that's because in order to reject something, we really have to think it is real, that it has power over us; for that we also really need to think both the thing rejected and the thing rejecting are real and lasting. The self is reified as both the subject and object! It's a sort of double whammy...

But we can receive something without thinking it is real, without clinging to it, as we do when watching a movie or reflecting on a dream...We must receive the individual self when we are off of the cushion in order to function in this world. But we can receive it, and everything else, with gentle, non-grasping hands...

2010
September Sesshin, Antaiji, Japan

... It again seemed clear to me sesshin can be seen as a sort of rehearsal for death, because in it all of life's toys are taken away. What will I do if/when faced with this "no toy" situation permanently? (if I get the luxury of contemplating my situation prior to the event called "death"). When its usual toys are taken away, the mind races around searching for things to play with: future plans, fantasies, regrets, etc. At most any given point, the end of sesshin seems an eternity away, so there is nothing to do but settle down into the moment. When I did settle like this, all was so peaceful; there was the rain and the cicadas and no human noise or interference. And yet I felt truly intimate with the middle-aged Japanese man who sat next to me. He seemed so solid yet so humble, always watching and waiting for others in order to see the right thing to do...Then there were the wind bells sounding in the typhoon that passed through. I couldn't help but think of Nyōjō Zenji's poem...

2011

ROHATSU SESSHIN, GYŌBUTSUJI

...One thing I seemed to continually face in this sesshin was the question, "Now, why am I sitting down again?"... Don joined me for every five-period morning block and for 10 periods of the last day. It was a great support. I really noticed how much difference it made to have him there. When I was alone, the option to simply quit seemed more real. Perhaps this is an important aspect this situation is teaching me, because this has never really seemed an option when others are present. I am too adept at being "a good boy," the one who always perseveres and anchors others with his steadfastness. But I really have to let go of that when I'm alone, of course. So why did I keep sitting down? I'm afraid part of the reason might have been that fears arose of having nothing real in my life: if I had no real practice, I had nothing to cling to, nothing to define me. Of course that is meaningless as a motivation for practice. That is just a toy. It's buying into the "possession game," a primary source of suffering. But as I continued, this motivation wasn't enough to keep me sitting down, because it became apparent it was a crutch. So it lost its power. I then couldn't help but see myself grasping for some reason to practice and searching for some validation as a human being. So it created a kind of crisis. If I didn't sit down, I would be pathetic because it would mean I don't have a genuine practice. It would mean I had founded this place and done all of that Zen training for nothing. And the alternative, to continue and sit down, just seemed the option to sit down into hell: aching shoulder muscles and endless hours of restless boredom. In the end I just kept sitting down for no real reason I can point to (this was the second day)....

I now come to the conclusion that when all is said and done, the sitting down is simply faith. It's strange because it's not the kind of faith l can call "mine", but rather a faith that just manifests, something that isn't personal. There's no way to intellectualize or take credit for it. It is the act of sitting down itself. At that desperate time I had two seemingly horrible choices to face over and over again: quit, go take a nap and feel like a loser, or sit down and endure the unendurable for countless hours. In the end, when faced with the moment, I simply sat down. I don't really know why or how. There was something going on beyond my understanding. ... I did finally settle into sesshin on the third day, and all the struggling stopped. ... It always seems so amazing when that happens.

2012
November Sesshin, Gyōbutsuji

... This morning it occurred to me that over the past two days since sesshin ended my mind is not ticking away in its usual manner. It's not, for example, licking the psychological wounds it thinks others have inflicted upon it. It has been difficult to see how often I indeed do this, however, how much of my energy has gone into "victimized" and judgmental thinking. Being here alone, I find surprisingly often my mind is caught up in thinking of how others have wronged me. But I notice, however, during the days immediately following sesshin little of this comes up, or at least I'm able to recognize it more quickly and let it go. This has nothing to do with any sort of personal achievement; it's the power of zazen. The hours spent in sesshin produce this effect, but all I have done is sit in the zendo doing nothing. There is no will or "self-power" involved.

After sesshin my heart is usually open and joyful; it feels a bit like Christmas Eve used to feel as a child, except there's not the focus on anticipation for receiving something. In fact, there is no anticipation at all, and I think this is key. It is pure joy in living.

I think this is at least partly due to a simple causal relationship: having been deprived of nearly all self-focused activity for some period, and then going back into normal life when that is finished. This is what I imagine returning from a "near-death experience" is like. There is appreciation for the simple things one takes for granted in everyday life. "You don't miss your water until your well runs dry."

Sawaki Rōshi did say doing zazen was like viewing your life from the grave, and I really understand that. And I do think it is more than just the deprivation/return effect. All of the letting go of thought for hours upon hours has some effect. I think the "habit links," the attachments to views, feeling and concepts that cause suffering, are in some way weakened. In zazen the attachment can actually be broken during the time of practice, although it sooner or later returns if we don't continue to practice with it in any particular moment. But directly following sesshin it always seems easier to let go of the habitual thought patterns and emotions. ...

After this sesshin I also feel more clarity around how the teachings of relative and absolute truth apply to direct experience. As Uchiyama Rōshi wrote, it is impossible to get through a sesshin utilizing only the force of one's will, and I think this is about giving up reliance solely on relative truths. When sitting down to a period of zazen while feeling bored and achy, if I think about the fact there are ten more periods to go in the day and three more days to go in the sesshin, that is facing the situation from a relative perspective. Comparing how many periods there are in one day or how many minutes there are left in this period is relative thinking. We have to use this kind of thinking, the measuring of time, to hold a sesshin. That is the only way we manage the schedule. But in the moment of sitting we let go of this relative measuring and sit in the absolute reality of the moment of "experience" (for lack of a better word). Actually, we let go of all notions of absolute reality, too. Here, in the eternity of the present, we are carried through the sesshin, and relative concerns are taken care of. So it is not that we favor the relative over the absolute, or the absolute over the relative, but we give up comparing them or distinguishing them from one another. Then the relative concerns, keeping the back straight, returning to the posture, and standing up when the bell rings, are expressions of absolute truth. And absolute truth, the total acceptance and non-grasping of all experience in the moment, takes care of relative truth, is not distinguishable from it. So letting go in zazen of concerns for the passing of time and concerns with attainment of enlightenment, is going beyond both relative and absolute truth.

MARCH SESSHIN, GYŌBUTSUJI

I felt sad most of this sesshin, but I was again shown that the cause of that sadness, whatever it was, was empty; by the fifth day the sun was out, my heart was calm, and I was feeling good.

Also on the fifth day I had that particular experience of practice joy that is not unusual for me on the last day of a sesshin. At that time I realized this joy is very simple; it involves quietly sitting and just feeling my skin, muscles, tissue, breath, heartbeat, etc. This is complete acceptance and joy in simply being—no measuring myself against how I think I should be or how others think I should be, no worries about money or unfinished projects. Though it is very simple, it is a deeply significant experience. It seems to me it's a glimpse of the actual life that lies beneath all of the superficial, conceptually based anxieties and preoccupations of a human being. Life is at its root OK and there is joy and worth in simply sitting down into it. ...

APRIL SESSHIN, GYŌBUTSUJI

[Note made before sesshin] It just occurred to me why sesshin can be such a difficult experience and yet simultaneously be so profound and joyful: it is at the same time the renunciation of all preferences but it is also the total renunciation of all sources of suffering. So it is difficult in that we give up all of the distractions and crutches we use to get through our lives, yet we also give up all of the things that cause us stress and difficulty. Often in fact, we confuse these two, but in sesshin we let all of them go so there is no need for the picking and choosing that is such a great source of stress and energy loss. ...

MAY SESSHIN, GYŌBUTSUJI

The first day or so of sesshin found my mind in a pretty sour place, with a lot of judgment coming up around people I thought had "wronged" me. But after a certain number of hours of sitting, I no longer had anything invested in those thoughts. It is truly amazing it's possible to let go of this type of suffering. Of course, some of those judgments may return, but in the past it seemed each time judgements came back, it was easier to see their conditioned nature, to see what had triggered them, and then let them go. And I often see the thoughts are arising almost randomly, with no connection to anything happening "outside of me" in the present. After all, I'm just sitting there doing nothing!

JUNE SESSHIN, GYŌBUTSUJI

... The primary thing I dealt with during this sesshin was the noise from the mushroom farm in the valley below us. I felt the old anger coming up. I think this was due as much to the fact that I have been enjoying a peaceful environment so much lately. The waterfalls have been running for several months, and I often sit at the southern falls in the mornings on my lighter practice days. The experience is incredibly beautiful and peaceful. ... So this illustrates how relativity is the source of my suffering. When I compare my present experience with some other experience, how things "could be" or "should be," for example, suffering arises. ...

129

... Sitting was very peaceful during times when the noise wasn't happening. At these times I couldn't help but notice I felt as if the mind was in harmony with zazen, yet when the noise came back, I felt the mind was not. But of course you can't measure the success of your zazen. The measuring of harmony, in fact, was probably what actually distanced me from zazen, if anything. Anger arising isn't such a problem if one doesn't cling to it. But measuring it against some other state of mind is the evidence that it is being reified. ...

And there is another perspective on this as well: there is the mirror of practice. I saw the mind is calm in calm circumstances, and it is agitated in agitated circumstances. Struggling with it to make it behave a certain way is just more agitation and distraction. So the key, of course, is to just keep letting go. Don't measure and don't identify. Just sit there. ...

JULY SESSHIN, GYŌBUTSUJI

... I received a rather difficult teaching from this sesshin. I realized I use the fact I am doing an intensive practice as a crutch, at least to a certain degree. ... It defines much of who I am, how I think of myself and maybe how I present myself to others. ... I realized how I was identifying with the "iron man" of zazen, the hardcore and unshakable sitter, and using it as a tool of my ego. I thought of how "naked" I felt after first arriving in Bloomington to practice at Sanshinji after my "crisis," after my ego seemed to have been torn to shreds by the difficulties I had just experienced. At that time I felt I had nothing to hold on to. It was very difficult but it actually felt very clean, too. Then of course my identity was repaired and rebuilt in order to function properly in the world, and the iron man was something created as a part of that process. I suppose it's not surprising, given the intensity of the style of practice I have done and continue to do. My ego was so happy to think it could do something perceived as difficult. For some time I have had some sense this had happened, but I hadn't seen it so clearly until this sesshin. Yet what would happen if I completely lost the iron man? What if I had some accident that prevented me from sitting at all? I would survive, keep going, and find some other way to practice, of course. But I will look at all of this more seriously. It's so clear that in order to face myself more deeply, to live and practice more sincerely, I must let go of clinging to the iron man.

... But I see in my present circumstances the iron man has been a comfort in a situation that is in many ways quite challenging and difficult. I'm practicing alone here at Gyōbutsuji for the most part, I have no local friends yet, and I'm still trying to figure out how to sustain this place financially. It's quite clear everything in my future is quite uncertain. (This is actually always so in any situation, of course.) The iron man has therefore been a support in a way, but I must be sure to see him for what he really is: a crutch and ultimately a hindrance. Besides, someday it will be very clear he can no longer exist; I'm not getting any younger.

I also had no "bliss periods" whatsoever during this sesshin. Just moment-to-moment practice. I have probably been secretly seeking those bliss periods that have arisen during the last several sesshins, but I have nonetheless tried to keep them in perspective. I think the bliss periods may have contributed to my clinging to the notion of the iron man, to tell you the truth. It is just more proof that taking those "special experiences" seriously is a dead end. ... Eventually, no matter how many of them I have, sooner or later I'm again faced with plain old Shōryū and all of his insecurities and foibles.

... I also saw clearly the conditioned and changing nature of my states of mind from another perspective. ... In the heat my whole being seemed to foul, and the clarity and lightness I did experience seemed only to arrive with cooler weather! No way to take any credit for "higher" states of mind, for sure. ... Of course, Uchiyama Rōshi wrote about this kind of observation. ...

SEPTEMBER SESSHIN, GYŌBUTSUJI

... So the first few days of sesshin were spent in this darkness of depression. Events and periods of my life kept coming up that "proved" my life has been a failure. It was a surprise this kind of suffering came up again at this point in my practice. ... I wondered, "What should I do with this?"

During sesshin there is ultimately nothing to do but sit down and let go of everything. So that's what I did; I just kept going the best I could. ... The past is irreversible and in sesshin the future seems to contain only more sitting, so there is nowhere to settle down but the immediate present. ...

So by the last day I found the darkness had lifted and I no longer saw myself as a worthless fool, as I had on day one. These states are amazing in that they seem so real, and yet they inevitably change. In sesshin this is really apparent since one is simply sitting quietly day in and day out, with few external distractions. There is nothing to do but face oneself and one's ever-changing sensations, emotions, and thoughts.

This letting go is so simple, yet so profound and important. It does not miraculously transform the mind in an instant, and it does not shape one into some sort of sage, but it can save us; it can bring us back to our sanity. It can allow us to remember life is worth fully embracing, and that it is such a precious gift.

2014

FEBRUARY SESSHIN, GYŌBUTSUJI

... Day four of sesshin was fine until the neighbor's dogs started barking in the evening. They just went on and on without a break, and I don't know when they stopped because they were still barking when I went to bed. That experience again triggered a very strong emotional response, including the thought that my chosen location for establishing Gyōbutsuji was completely wrong. I felt the impulse to simply quit sesshin, and it even occurred to me to walk away from the entire way of life I've been trying to establish here. I just wanted to give up. For some reason, those dogs barking triggered this extremely strong emotional response. I told myself if they were barking again the next night, I would skip the two evening periods.

I woke up with the same dark mind the next morning. It was the first time I can remember ever having started the fifth day on a bad note. That morning I felt no sense of joy; the day ahead seemed as if it might as well have been another five days. I had no will to sit, but I just sat down anyway. The periods of zazen dragged on. Then, amazingly, during the second or third period after breakfast, I experienced some sort of internal, perhaps physical shift. It happened very quickly. It was as if suddenly the clouds of my mind and body broke and the sun shone through. There was no more darkness, no more loathing of my situation. I decided later to keep sitting in the evening, dogs or no dogs. I would just practice with whatever was there. ... It was clear this shift had nothing whatsoever to do with my individual effort. Perhaps it was simply some sort of physiological imbalance returning to normal. ...

MARCH SESSHIN, GYŌBUTSUJI

... It became very apparent during sesshin there is no real reason to look forward to future events. This is in line with well-known Buddhist principles, and it's easy to see and accept in theory, but I imagine for most people, surely for myself, this theory is not so easily adopted as everyday practice. Feeling the hours and days creep by so slowly but nonetheless ultimately pass really brings this simple reality into the realm of direct experience. I think about the ways I look forward to things at the end of the week, perhaps a night of reading or watching a documentary of some sort, and I then realize the moments of enjoyment just pass and are gone. I think about their coming for days, perhaps, but their passing takes only an hour or two, some just moments. More time is spent in anticipation than in actual enjoyment. Nothing can be held. I have lived much of my life, I think, trying to manipulate conditions in order to encounter enjoyable circumstances and avoid distasteful ones. The enjoyable event or situation arrives and then passes, but are things ultimately really ever any different? Sometimes I can answer "yes" in some limited way, as when I feel rested after a nice light day, but the fundamental issue of living, of "what is all of this and how do I respond to it?" has not changed. Any good mood or feeling always changes, and I'm back into the cycle of chasing conditions once more. Is that any foundation for a meaningful life? ... Somehow this simple truth seems to have been driven home during this sesshin. ...

[Later in the entry; topic has changed] Since finishing sesshin I've been thinking about the relationship between "opening the hand of thought" and "being one" with one's experience. During zazen the point is not to separate, of course, from any experience, but the term "letting go" has a bit of that connotation, of separation. I suppose we emphasize letting go of thinking since people are so prone to grasp their thoughts, and thinking has such a profound experience on how we feel and behave. And yet I remember the original Japanese word Uchiyama Rōshi used in this phrase includes emotions, preferences, and sensations. I think it is essential we let go of feelings and sensations in zazen. But of course that does not mean we reject them. I think the point I'm sorting out is that feelings in the body and emotional states actually become more acute in sitting; somehow letting them go allows one to experience them more fully. This is a known principle, of course, but the implications are quite amazing. I think it implies being one with one's experience means we let go of our experience, we just let it be. I believe the tendency, however, is to consider "being one" with something as involving intense concentration or effort, but I don't believe that is the case. ... By focusing on something we can actually distort our perception of it and even grasp it. So perhaps "departing from the five skandhas," a key teaching of the Buddha, is synonymous with being one with the skandhas; another way of talking about both opening the hand and "being one with" might be "going beyond union or separation."...

JUNE SESSHIN, GYŌBUTSUJI

... More intense suffering came up during this sesshin. It was centered around a difficult interaction with someone who had visited recently, and it involved me being displeased with his behavior. I thought a pretty good relationship had been developing with this person, and part of my intention for the behavior was to allow for deeper communication and genuine practice. ... But the interaction did not go well, I think, and it only created a gulf between us. Anyway, during zazen I got to mulling over all of this and the narrative came up that I'm an angry person who can't sustain a relationship involving any amount of intimacy. The mind went on and on like this within this extreme narrative. I'm still feeling a bit bruised this morning, honestly speaking. It's strange this happened on the fourth day, since in my experience this is usually a time when my emotional suffering has already dropped away. As a result of this episode coming up so late, the suffering probably wasn't fully released by the end of sesshin. ...

As I now reflect a bit more, I do realize I don't know this person so well. I thought he was at a place in his practice where he was willing to see himself more genuinely and take responsibility for his mistakes, but I actually don't know if that is so. I'm finding people are usually more sensitive than one would expect. ... I must always look carefully to see how to best respond to each individual in each particular situation. ...

2015
MARCH SESSHIN, GYŌBUTSUJI

... I noted on the third day a desire for a special experience arising in zazen. It's disappointing to see it again, but there it was. I just kept letting go of it and did my best to stay present. But immediately after sesshin I found myself thinking about the concrete nature of "enlightenment." Of course I understand the ultimate view of Dōgen's teaching on enlightenment, but he did also talk about conventional "improvement" in practice, especially in *Zuimonki*, for example. And I must admit I can't help wanting to become better at practicing with anger when it arises, for instance. Perhaps this is the kind of improvement he was speaking of. It seems a more conventional or "gradual" approach to practice, a sort of complementary perspective to "practice and enlightenment are one." But I do understand he didn't separate the two perspectives; they are really one thing. ... Each "stage" of practice is total realization when fully engaged.

... But will I ever come to a place and think, "Finally, I have good mastery over my emotional responses"? Isn't this what I really hope for? Isn't this, at least on some level, the kind of thinking that keeps us working on the gradual path? Perhaps we realize we can't achieve perfection, but we do, nonetheless, see some improvement.

In a moment of letting go of anger, the "goal" is realized. This is the meaning of "practice and enlightenment are one." But of course the anger comes back and we have to deal with it again. ... Within my relationships at Sanshinji I worked much with my anger responses, and I made some genuine discoveries concerning the conditioning of my emotions and even real "progress" in handling those habits ... but disappointments have again arisen, and I imagine they will always arise to some degree. There is always more work to do, more depth to explore. And although reflection on my past behavior is necessary, the key is to face each encounter with 100% of my heart/mind/body in the present, not fretting over future outcomes or past mistakes. That is the only way to come to terms with the past, present, and future. I believe this is Dōgen Zenji's concrete instruction for moment-to-moment realization.

... But I will give a talk soon on "faith," for example, and I want to be able to encourage others on this subject. So I do want to be clear about my own faith, practice and realization of the teachings around the sudden and gradual aspects of Dōgen Zenji's teaching. ... It seems so important to be able to provide experientially-based guidance on these teachings. ... I think people find little use in them if they are approached simply as theories or ideas. ... This is a fundamental reason to aspire to improve on a conventional level, as far as I can see. I think this is true vow being nurtured. ... Perhaps the most sincere reason to hope for "progress" is to attain the experience and ability to encourage others. ...

JULY SESSHIN, GYŌBUTSUJI

... [Discussing a certain state of mind in zazen] In this "experience of freedom" I had on the fifth day, I knew I, and everyone else in the world, was OK. It was a release from what I understand to be the fundamental burden that plagues a human being. I understood all people are just trying to get by as best they can, and no one is ultimately better or worse than anyone else. We are all just limited little creatures trying to make our way. There is no ultimate judgement that can assign worth to us or take worth away. We are all just part of life, part of some vastly huge reality we can't fully comprehend. Everything is just ultimately OK. It felt so light, joyful and free. ...

137

It was clear my individual effort had nothing to do with the dropping away of my fundamental suffering. It just happened. It was as if the zazen posture was somehow temporarily letting the suffering drip down from my body and mind. ... This state of mind was conditioned and impermanent, but I believe it has been useful to me as part of the scenery of zazen: by contrasting it with states of suffering, it shows the emptiness and conditioned nature of all states, illustrating how these states eventually change, no matter how much we like them or think they are real or true. ... But the "freedom state" is obviously not more genuine or real than states of suffering. That is important to remember. Otherwise pursuing this experience becomes the object of practice, and that of course is just more samsara.

September Sesshin, Gyōbutsuji

Today I do have the feeling sesshin has cleaned a lot of extra mental debris away. Things are clearer and in better perspective. Life is simpler than one thinks. ... Sesshin is a great teacher in that way. It shows us we can settle down and see how much simpler things are than we usually imagine.

... I had a lot of musings coming up about death. Interesting. As I always say, sesshin is itself a kind of death. It is the letting go of all of our usual toys and props. But when that final letting-go comes, will I be present enough to sincerely practice during that event? Lately it has seemed clearer it just doesn't matter so much when my death does come. Sooner or later we all have to face it. What difference does 30, 20, 10 years, or 1 year, make, really? In the overall picture, in the timelessness of "eternity," isn't it all the same? Ultimately perhaps the only truly valid reason for wanting to postpone death is to have more time to fulfill the offerings one can give. I suppose this is a part of the bodhisattva vow. It's OK to be attached to this life, or at least to accept the fact that we are attached when the attachment is supporting our vow. ...

2016
JANUARY SESSHIN, GYŌBUTSUJI

This was the first sesshin the new resident and I had done alone together. It was intimate in many ways, but some of those ways were difficult. ... I am still continuing to learn what it means to give without expectation. Will I ever be able to truly do this? Is anyone able? It seems there must always be on some level some expectation when one gives. And yet the ability to let go of the expectations and the related disappointments does seem to increase with time. I think that comes when we receive the expectation, accept it, and let it go over and over again (as we do in zazen). Then perhaps someday we will notice some expectations have disappeared, but if we look with expectation for lack of expectation, that is a problem! ... It is in zazen where we truly do let go of all expectations and agendas ... but I imagine one is always discovering new ways delusion is created in daily life beyond the zendo. I do know, of course, any difficult emotion or narrative is ultimately my own illusion. But we have to "go with" the illusion sometimes, treat it as if it were real, in order to get things done in this life. Of course the point is to stay aware that one is simply "going with the illusion." Then one can stay clearer and is less likely to create suffering. It is when we really believe in the illusion that we get caught and are dragged around by illusions and personal narratives.

MARCH SESSHIN, GYŌBUTSUJI

... [Discussing a mental state] But I noticed this beneficent state is quite contingent on the mind's interpretation of how I am perceived by others. If the mind feels it is being treated fairly, with respect and admiration, it is quite a gentle and forgiving mind. If it feels it is being disparaged and judged, it will have the impulse to disparage, judge, and seek blame.

This might seem quite natural, but of course in reality it is not so good. Does the mind ever come to a place where it can feel kind and non-judging, even when it feels it is possibly being judged? The challenge, of course, is to let go not only of one's thoughts and judgements about self and other, but also to let go of the perception that one is misunderstood or being judged unfairly, even if there is evidence this judgement is actually happening on some level. I find it very difficult to let go of my own judgements concerning the perceived misguided judgements of others. Letting go does not mean I don't use certain information in discerning a best course of action, but letting go of belief in my judgements is the only thing that can leave room for a gentle and forgiving mind. I think this is Dōgen Zenji's magnanimous mind, and it arises of its own accord when we let go of clinging to our experience, including judgements.

April Sesshin, Gyōbutsuji

After much anticipation on my part, a person who had for months been planning to come for sesshin didn't arrive. Some sort of last-minute mistake prevented her arrival. I found out while shopping on the day she was scheduled to arrive. We had been pretty concerned about making her comfortable, and we put some additional stress on ourselves as we made preparations. But in the end the worry and stress were just wasted energy. So here's another lesson in simply facing reality as it comes, rather than anticipating problems (and creating them) before they actually present themselves. It is amazing to see how many of the problems I encounter are mostly fabrications of my mind. I imagine a large part of people's suffering arises due to this kind of self-created stress that is much more intense than the stress created by "external" conditions. ...

[Later in the entry, a change of subject] So much judgement, projection, and annoyance the mind can conjure up in its silence! Yet just as I suspected, when we begin talking again, the reality of interacting often lets the judgmental mind drop. It is true, of course, that we drop all judgement and projection in zazen. But I think it is important to note that silence can be fertile ground for a raging, deluded mind. The reality of who we think a person is can be quite different according to whether we are silent or when we are interacting verbally. The mind is very good at projecting undesirable behaviors and thoughts on others. In this kind of monastic-practice environment, we have the rare opportunity to check our projections against the reality of the person we encounter, providing an environment of trust and sincerity has been established. Also, practitioners need to be sincere and motivated enough to delve into this seemingly risky territory. I think this is part of the fearlessness of the bodhisattva. ...

2017
JANUARY 2017 SESSHIN, GYŌBUTSUJI

... [Discussing a state experienced in zazen] I suppose one could say this "everything is OK experience" is the mind adopting the absolute perspective. I think there is a tendency to think there is some "absolute principle or nature of reality" beyond our experience, but I find I have little interest in that perspective these days. More and more I want to apply the teachings of the Two Truths simply to the reality of here and now. What else do we have, anyway, other than direct experience? All else in just imagination or conjecture.

... I understand why we tend to prefer the experience of what we think of as this "absolute perspective" of the mind, this place of peace and oneness. It is so nice to have its residual effects inform our life off of the cushion, too. But I think there is actually a danger in feeling this kind of peace for extended periods. One can get to a place of wanting to simply hang out in this bliss and do nothing but enjoy the lack of suffering. But if we are to really live by vow, I think we have to connect with the pain again, and in any case, it sooner or later becomes inevitable, actually, whether we want to do it or not. Receiving our pain allows us to do something for others and in turn do something for ourselves. It's just that we must avoid investing so much of ourselves in the dark stories. It's all in the way we practice with the darkness. We mustn't believe in it, just as we mustn't ultimately believe everything is OK. How can I really think everything is OK, when I know there are children living on heaps of garbage in India? But if we identify too much with our own painful stories or stories about the pain of others, those stories suck away all of our energy. ...

So in a way, the absolute and relative perspectives create some kind of balance that fortifies life. Sticking to either perspective produces some sort of lack or surfeit that freezes up our ability to live and act productively and wholesomely. ...

April Sesshin, Gyōbutsuji

... The day following sesshin I thought there had been none of the usual "redemption" from the dark thoughts and emotions that had arisen. However, at some point I realized I was feeling so sensitive and quietly joyful in hearing the spring peepers and feeling the wind on my face as I stood outside. So here I am at "home" again after all, with everything around me reminding me this present is the only real redemption, the ultimate refuge. Fluctuations in emotions and the mind are, in the end, not so important, and there's really no absolute or relative perspective when one simply settles down in the here-and-now.

I also realized the preciousness of this sensitive, unique world I live in. For so much of my life, I have thought of it as weakness, this sensitivity. But it is a gift, if I receive it and honor it as such. ... All too often, it seems, we human beings find ourselves engulfed in a subjective world of anger or resentment, so when this world of the boy-with-his-heart-on-his-sleeve manifests, shouldn't I receive it as a sublime gift? The mistake is to believe in it as an objective, enduring reality beyond my own world of experience, of course; I can't expect others to endorse it or even understand it. Perhaps, however, I will always hope and even search, in some way, for another human being who can understand and honor it. This kind of longing is fundamental to the human experience, I think: to be truly seen and met by another human being. ... But actually finding the connection is not the primary point. The longing, perhaps, is simply part of the life energy that fuels our expression of vow. In fact, one can never be truly fulfilled, of course, by any person or any thing "outside." It is so important to understand this; otherwise our longing simply triggers chasing after fantasies as a way to escape facing the truth of here-and-now. It is especially important to understand we won't ever truly find a deep connection with others if we are seeking that connection in order to simply fulfill our longing or desire. I have long known I can't seek redemption in someone else. Still, one must admit and face the longing. Grasping is bound to happen if it is shunned or denied. This longing can be the source of compassion, I think, if held in a certain way. It can actually be fulfilled in many ways other than romantic connection. ... We humans want connection and respect from the "outside," but finding it from a deeper source is even harder; it's impossible, in fact, if we use our usual seeking methods. But this source is the only font of real peace. Of course, this "source" is simply our practice. It's not a static "source" in the usual sense of the word. ...

Rohatsu Sesshin, Gyōbutsuji

... A simple but profound insight hit home again concerning the bodhisattva vow. I again realized that the reason we don't strive to become buddhas is that we are living to make all people buddha, to make our shared lives buddha; that is the essence of my teacher's interpretation of the first bodhisattva vow as all beings staying on this shore of samsara, while saying "you first," instead of leaving for the other shore of nirvana. This strikes me as another way to express what Shakyamuni said when he looked up at the morning star: "I and all beings together attain the way."

So how can I strive to make this person a buddha when I realize a buddha expressing buddhahood on his/her own is such a deep fiction? Shakyamuni saw it; perhaps it was the essence of the "flower joke" that passed between him and Mahakasyapa. This is the way I want to express the essence of what it means to live genuinely, to live by vow.

CHAPTER EIGHT

HŌKŌ KARNEGIS

How the West was Won:
Shaping the landscape
of the 21st-century bodhisattva

Every year when I file my annual activity report with Sōtōshū, I look back through calendars and Facebook pages and photo files to glean a list and set of images of the many opportunities I've had over the previous 12 months to carry out my bodhisattva vows. It's my report, but it's not just me in the photos and I'm not sitting in empty space—there's a zendo full of practitioners or a meeting table ringed with committee members or a classroom full of local residents who know nothing as yet about Buddhism and have no idea that they are bodhisattvas. Somehow causes and conditions have resulted in all of us fetching up here at one time on the shore of the dharma. The karma of the 21st-century West has made use of everything at its disposal—from the internet to global events to European philosophy to interstate and international travel—to bring us together and to bring us to Zen.

However, the Zen we encounter and practice doesn't look like the Zen of our ancestors. We don't share the same karmic conditions and the differences in space, time and culture have wrought real change in the way we in the West understand their teachings. We've intentionally and unintentionally made changes by mixing in elements of the surrounding Judeo-Christian environment and leaving out traditional Asian elements that don't make sense to us. Over time, deliberate modifications have also been made in an attempt to tailor Buddhism or Zen specifically to modern American sensibilities, aligning with the interests of our particular society at a particular time in order to create a more perfect fit. From Victorian Buddhist apologists in the West to Japanese promoters of Zen in the age of World War II, significant effort has been made to downplay historic, cultural, or traditional elements that might turn Westerners off, and bring to the fore the elements that could be positioned as aligning with and enhancing our existing attitudes and goals.

These changes can't help but affect the way we understand our work as bodhisattvas and the tools and opportunities we have to carry it out. And yet, isn't there supposed to be something universal about Zen, something that is not bound by the constraints of culture and worldview and institutions that some would say have attached themselves like barnacles to a once pure and simple dharma? After all, our zazen and awakening are said to be the same as Buddha's zazen and awakening, and he sat 25 centuries ago on the other side of the world. Shouldn't our bodhisattva vows be more about the lotus that rises above the water than about the samsaric mud in which its roots are mired?

In one way, as we make and carry out our vows it's important to recognize the particular nature of contemporary Western suffering. In another, it's not important at all. Human suffering is and has always been based on the delusion of the existence of a separate, fixed, and unchanging self. In the last hundred years we've gone from Brownie cameras and phonographs to smartphones and digital music, but the stories we're telling ourselves about the nature of self haven't changed all that much. The pattern of the arising of suffering and our liberation from it is part of the human condition and is one of the commonalities that connect us across space and time.

At the same time, we are the products of our culture and our times, playing out our particular karma as we do our best to help others to play out their own karma in the most skillful and wholesome way. As bodhisattvas, we use the elements of our conditioned existence—the time, place, culture, and other circumstances of our birth as well as our particular personal skills and abilities—to carry out the work of liberation. Thus it's critically important that we recognize and examine the assumptions we take into that work, ideas we take for granted about our culture, Japanese culture, our collective history, and the ways in which contemporary Western practice has shifted in focus and approach from traditional Asian practice as we attempt to create something that works for us here and now.

In the realm of personal vow, I've always aspired to stand in the intersection between tradtional and modern practice and between East and West. My own practice has been and continues to be an exploration of the relationship between the forms that support us in our human condition as we aim toward manifesting our awakening and the universal elements of Zen and awakening that do not rely on those forms, interesting and comforting though they may be. In this chapter I will explore the tension between the life of the bodhisattva as a conditioned being moving through a conditioned world of practice and the urge to decontextualize practice and vow from those conditioned circumstances in an effort to get to a "pure essence" of Zen and awakening that is universally applicable to the work of liberating all beings.

THE CONDITIONED WORLD OF PRACTICE

The conditioned world is a world of continuous change. The skillful bodhisattva knows that while he or she may carry a particular vow for a lifetime, not only will his or her skills develop and change, the needs of beings vary and a vast array of dharma gates come and go, but elements of the practice itself will shift and transform across time and space. In some cases the changes that have happened in Buddhism and Zen have been the outcome of Western misinterpretation and misunderstanding of Asian traditions. In others it's been the result of syncretism, the combining of different elements of religion or culture. In still others the repackaging has been entirely deliberate in order to appeal to a particular audience. As David McMahon points out, "What many Americans and Europeans often understand by the term 'Buddhism' . . . is actually a modern hybrid tradition with roots in the European Enlightenment no less than the Buddha's enlightenment, in Romanticism and transcendentalism as much as the Pali canon, and in the clash of Asian cultures and colonial powers as much as in mindfulness and meditation. Most non-Asian Americans tend to see Buddhism as a religion whose most important elements are meditation, rigorous philosophical analysis, and an ethic of compassion combined with a highly empirical psychological science that encourages reliance on individual experience. It discourages blindly following authority and dogma, has little place for superstition, magic, image worship, and gods, and is largely compatible with the findings of modern science and liberal democratic values. While this picture draws on elements of traditional forms of Buddhism that have existed for centuries, it is in many respects distinct from what Buddhism has meant to Asian Buddhists throughout its long and varied history." [1]

This is important for us as we offer our practice in the world as a means of ameliorating suffering. Familiarity with Buddhist history and canonical texts can lead us to believe that the Zen we practice today in the 21st-century is at its core exactly that of our ancestors over the centuries. Sure, maybe we chant in English, and maybe the average Zen center doesn't look like a *senmon sōdō* or training temple in Japan, and maybe we've put aside some of the more "supernatural" elements of the tradition, but haven't zazen, mindfulness, and enlightenment always been what Zen is about? Aren't we essentially carrying on the practice of our ancestors just as it's been transmitted to us?

The fact is that many of the values, teachings, and activities that we take for granted as being at the heart of our Sōtō Zen practice have not always been so, or at least not in their current forms. What we rely on in carrying out our vows is a new tradition of modern Western Sōtō Zen created from a combination of old and new, East and West.

This puts before us both opportunities and challenges. Adapting teachings and practice to the times and places in which we live may perhaps make them more accessible to a wider range of people. It may also cause us to misintepret them, make assumptions about their context and meaning, and act on the basis of those misunderstandings in a well-meaning attempt to help others in the belief that we are offering ancient truths unaltered by anyone's agenda or personal or cultural filters.

THE CLASH OF CULTURES

When Europeans visited and explored Buddhist sites in India in the 18th century, they found places of residential practice. These they called "monasteries," and the residents "monks." They saw someone heading up the community. This they called an "abbot." They saw respected practitioners teaching and leading practice. These they called "priests." This Christian terminology is with us to this day, born of the only frame of reference available to these explorers and only marginally accurate in its description of Buddhist practice.

Of course, these Europeans weren't the first to try to understand Buddhism according to their own frame of reference or fit it into a cultural container in which things didn't match up. As Buddhism traveled down the Silk Road in the second century BCE, it encountered cultures very different from that of the India in which it originated. The Chinese, for example, valued responsibility to family, clan, state, and emperor, while Buddhism encouraged practitioners to leave home for a mendicant life in the sangha. To a Chinese, to leave home, cut ties, and give up work was to default completely and shamefully on societal obligations. While Indian monks did not engage in work and relied on donations from the laity for their subsistence, Chinese monks made daily work a central element of their practice. Cultural clashes like these, combined with the difficulties of translating Sanskrit and Pali texts into a pictographic language that had no equivalent terms for some of the concepts, changed the teachings and practice. For instance, when Buddhist "emptiness" arrived in China it was taken to be the same as the "nothingness" of the pre-existing Daoist tradition. The misinterpretation did not become apparent for several hundred years.

In more modern times, in the search for a way to describe awakening, Western cultures steeped in European philosophy adopted the word "Enlightenment" as comparable to terms like *bodhi*, *kensho* or *satori*. "Enlightenment" is rooted in an intellectual movement of the late 17th and 18th centuries emphasizing reason and individualism over tradition. In common English usage the word has a connotation of intellectual knowledge or wisdom and usually implies a state of being. All this, of course, is not at all what Dōgen teaches us is the nature of Buddha's awakening.

150

SYNCRETISM

The syncretic merging of various beliefs and practices from the surrounding culture into Zen carries no misunderstanding and no intention or agenda; changes happen simply because two or more cultures or traditions meet on the same soil and practitioners add new elements that appeal to them or interpret Zen according to their own karmic circumstances. For instance, studies have shown that Americans who have converted to Buddhism tend to be more egalitarian, liberal, well-educated, and affluent than others, and are predominantly white.[2] Those characteristics, naturally, have shaped choices about what activities to include, how to organize and lead sanghas, what teachings to emphasize and how to interpret them, leading to a style of practice that may look quite different from its Asian counterparts.

Joshua Irizarry points out that early American Zen enthusiasts tended to fall into three types: wealthy and stylish conspicuous consumers, artists and creatives, and spiritual seekers looking to replace or supplement institutionalized religion. "To each of these groups, Zen was a mirror which reflected that which was most desired. To the group of fashionable conspicuous consumers, integrating Japanese and 'Zen' aesthetic elements into design, fashion and high culture granted an aura of class, cosmopolitanism, and sophistication. For the artists such as the Beat Poets, Zen lent itself to ideals of creativity, spontaneity, altered consciousness, social protest, and irreverence for established authority. To the spiritual seekers, Zen was positioned as a traditional, but non-religious 'philosophy' or 'practice' free from doctrine, ritual, and hierarchy."[3] The worldviews that go with these lifestyles have provided the background for the development of a uniquely American Sōtō Zen, created from the elements that feel most comfortable and reinforce pre-existing values.

Americans are increasingly moving away from the mainstream Judeo-Christian traditions in which they may have been raised or by which they've been surrounded, yet they may still feel the need for spirituality in their lives. Younger people in particular are searching not so much for a religious tradition as for a set of "spiritual technologies," practices or elements they can pick and choose and add to their lives to create a personalized container and worldview that works for them. One study has showed that nearly a third of American Buddhists say they are affiliated with more than one religion.[4]

VICTORIAN BUDDHISM

The latest information from Gallup shows that Americans believe the most important problems at the moment are dissatisfaction with the government, race relations, healthcare, unifying the country and immigration. Just slightly farther down the list are lack of respect for one another and the decline of ethics, morality, religion, and the family. This is the landscape through which the American bodhisattva walks today.

A century ago, the issues at hand were things like whether or not to enter World War I, corruption in business and politics, women's suffrage, prohibition, child labor and the question of "hyphenated Americans"—those who had immigrated from other countries and continued to display loyalty to their homelands as German-Americans, Irish-Americans, etc. Industrialization and urbanization were leading to alienation as social relationships were cut off. Nineteenth-century bodhisattvas in the US were dealing with different permutations of the issues we still face today—and Buddhism was beginning to take hold in America as a new way to respond to suffering.

Buddhism as studied and practiced in America was bound to be shaped by the cultural elements already in place when it began to emerge in the Victorian era. At the beginning, Americans looked askance at Buddhism as a pessimistic and passive tradition. Traits like these were in direct conflict with the prevalent optimism and activism of the day, which held that life in this benevolent universe was getting better and had the potential for continued progress and development with a suitable application of effort to uplift people and society. Leaders pointed to the end of the Civil War and Reconstruction, scientific and technological progress, American territorial expansion, and a belief in the country's role as a "Redeemer Nation" as affirmations of this optimistic outlook. Theism and individualism were also held in high regard in a largely Christian culture. By contrast, Buddhism seemed to be determined to negate all of these: there was no God and no self, life was characterized by suffering, and practitioners did all they could to sit quietly and detach themselves from the world. If it was going to get a foothold and make a dent in 19th-century suffering, adherents and sympathizers were going to have to position Buddhism in a way that was acceptable in its new surroundings, appealing to Rationalists and Romantics alike.

This they did by calling out the aspects of Buddhism that could be seen as optimistic and active. For instance, the Buddha was a reformer, they asserted, with a deeply-held code of ethics and a belief in equal treatment for all, offering a way out of suffering and a means of liberation based on one's own efforts. For Rationalists, who made their way to religious truth through investigation rather than revelation, karmic law was equated with the natural forces of evolution and teachings of no-self were positioned as consistent with the new science of psychology. For Romantics, the need for imagination, aesthetics and exoticism was supplied by Buddhism's association with Eastern cultures and arts. The cultural shift from reliance on external authorities such as religious institutions in determining truth to reliance on internal reflection and experience was accommodated by

HOW THE WEST WAS WON

moving meditation practice to the center of the tradition. Buddhism was adapted to make it consistent and compatible with as much of the Victorian American worldview as possible.

A CASE IN POINT: THE NEW CENTRALITY OF "MEDITATION"

It surprises many Westerners to learn that "meditation" has not always been the main occupation of all Buddhist practitioners. Historically, it was the domain of specialist monks; there were similarly specialists in texts or in rituals. "While meditation has always been considered essential to awakening and is respected and revered in most Buddhist communities the representation of it as the sine qua non of Buddhist practice for monastics and laity alike is largely a modern development and a key constituent of Buddhist modernism," McMahon writes.[5]

Within late-1800s Sōtō Zen in Japan, although zazen was considered the focus of practice as handed down by Dōgen, it was thought to be too arduous an activity for the average layperson. When the sect sought to expand and solidify its base, it did so not through spreading the practice of zazen, but by developing and offering a way for laity to take precepts and by compiling and distributing the *Shushōgi*, a heavily-edited selection of Dōgen's main teaching points. Despite this, there are a number of reasons that zazen has moved to the front and center of practice in the West. Sitting practice, while considered essential, is seen as easy to separate from its Buddhist context and tradition, such that it becomes universal and can be applied to the achievement of personal goals. When viewed through the lens of Romantic philosophy, it aligns with the value placed on private experience over the teachings and structures of an institution and the movement away from external authority and toward a rich interior life. Zazen seems to offer a means of working with the Romantic tension between the primacy of the individual and the search for cosmic unity and meaning. On the other hand, the positioning of Buddhism as rational and scientific has led Westerners to see zazen and practice through the lens of psychology as a spiritual technology that can be used for mental and physical health. The advent of "book culture" allowed anyone access to written zazen instructions, not just the specialist monks who could read rare texts and learn from masters, and these days the Buddhist publishing industry is booming.

These lenses help to explain the ideas and preconceptions that new practitioners bring with them into that first zazen instruction session. Likely some of them are there to reduce their stress. Others are engaged in a search for meaning. Still others want to become more creative or improve their focus in the workplace. All of these are expressions of dissatisfaction, the *dukkha* that the Buddha came to understand with his own awakening and spent his life trying to help others dissolve. Those new practitioners are probably not there to manifest their Buddha nature. They're there to deal with what they perceive as the discomfort of modern Western life. The skillful bodhisattva recognizes this and offers guidance to move them toward an understanding that "zazen is good for nothing."

THE UNIVERSAL PRACTICE

Zen practice in the West now includes a significant number of practitioners who think of themselves as ecumenical or secular Buddhists, or as nonadherents to any tradition at all. There are those who value the devotional elements, the bodhisattvas, and the liturgy, and there are those who simply want to work for their own awakening, which they see as a universal experience outside of any religious context. Looking back, we can discern several forces, both Asian and Western, which have converged to support this shift.

The first is the universalization of Zen awakening. In the mid-20th century, Japanese lay scholar D. T. Suzuki was instrumental in positioning Zen in a way that would be acceptable to Westerners, a project undertaken to position post-WWII Japan as a modern, powerful nation, and its culture as refined and superior in the face of Western hegemony. Suzuki sought to remove Zen from its cultural context and make it accessible and applicable to everyone. This extraction cut its ties to monks and monasteries, the precepts, sangha life, rituals and teachings, and set up instead an individual internal experience as the only reliable "truth." Positioning Zen as based on the truth of an ineffable personal experience protected it from rejection as superstition or the creation of a backward or bewildered community.

At the same time, it could not be replaced by science or rationalism because the awakening experience was said to be subjective. It was beyond all the limitations of organized sects, cultural manifestations, political exigencies, or other karmic conditions. As Robert Sharf explains, "The notion of 'pure Zen'—a pan-cultural religious experience unsullied by institutional, social, and historical contingencies—would be attractive precisely because it held out the possibility of an alternative to the godless and indifferent anomic universe bequeathed by the Western Enlightenment, yet demanded neither blind faith nor institutional allegiance. This reconstructed Zen offered an intellectually reputable escape from the epistemological anxiety of historicism and pluralism."[5]

With increasingly global communication, Western practice has been influenced by a Southeast Asian movement known as "Protestant Buddhism," which picks up on the assertion that each person is responsible for his own awakening, seeking that goal without the help of intermediaries such as clergy or deities. This awakening happens not in a monastery or temple amidst monks and nuns, but in the everyday world. Protestant Buddhism was a response to the British colonialism of the 1800s, under which emphasis was placed on converting the population to Christianity. A Buddhist revitalization movement that had been influenced by that very Christianity emerged later in the century; it sought to curb the growing economic and religious power of religious institutions. The result was an emphasis on each practitioner's ability and responsibility to gain the self-understanding that leads to his or her own awakening. What became important was not the public activity that happened within the ordained sangha, but what happened in the individual heart and mind.

INDIVIDUAL AND UNIVERSAL AWAKENING

When I was teaching Eastern Religion in the college classroom, I explained to my students the difference between ethnic and universal religions. Ethnic religions had no ambition to spread themselves beyond the immediate group or area in which they arose, while universal religions were willing to transmit their teachings to everyone everywhere. We discussed Hinduism and Shintō as examples of ethnic religions that may travel across the world with their adherents but have not had an influx of converts from outside of their originating cultures. Buddhism, on the other hand, we discussed as an example of a universal religion, one that appealed to people across cultures and geographic locations.

The universal nature of Zen lies in both the microcosm of the karmically-conditioned individual and the macrocosm of One Unified Reality. If the core activity of our practice is the awakening of each individual sentient being and, as Dōgen says, all sentient beings are Buddha-nature, then it doesn't matter where we encounter them or under what circumstances; as bodhisattvas we are responsible for assisting them in that awakening, and as Buddha-nature itself they are all already awake. While their karmic circumstances may differ, each individual has suffering, whether Asian, Western, Victorian, modern, practicing Buddhist or not. There is no individual we are not responsible for helping and no individual that doesn't need our help.

Our practice and vow is also universal from the broad standpoint of the nature of reality. Buddha's way is said to be unsurpassable because there is nothing outside of it. The deep and nonseperate recognition of human suffering, its cause and the means to free ourselves and all beings from it penetrates everywhere. It's not confined to one place or time and we can't escape. We can practice wisdom, ethics, and concentration through the elements of the Eightfold Path wherever we are and whomever we're with.

THE INTERSECTION OF KARMA AND VOW

The story of Buddhism and Zen is, of course, still unfolding, and it's a complex and fascinating tale. This chapter has touched on a few examples and major developments but can in no way be exhaustive. Suffice it to say that Western Sōtō Zen practitioners function within a complex karmic context of which many are likely unaware; the danger in this is that practitioners may believe that while naturally minor changes have occurred as Zen has spread across time and space, the practice of the modern West emphasizes the same things as that of our ancestors and that we are seeing the teachings without the inherent distortion that comes with cultural filters. If we as bodhisattvas are to apply the teachings to the liberation of beings, it's critical that we see our own assumptions and know that we may be reading a different intention into the writings of our ancestors than they intended. This is one of the reasons that the work of teachers and translators like Okumura Rōshi is so vital to the development of Western Sōtō Zen. We must learn from those who can truly get inside the tradition in a way that we cannot—not from lack of desire or intention, but because our karmic conditioning has caused us to be born into another culture. We may not pick up on the literary allusions and cultural cues embedded in a text written by Dōgen for monks in a training temple in medieval Japan and may instead interpret that text according to our modern Western sensibilities, with less than optimal results.

The recognition of the universality of human suffering that is at the heart of our practice would seem to indicate that there is also a universal set of Buddhist values that transcends culture, and that all practitioners hold the same views about what's important. Indeed, the West makes great effort to promote its values of democracy and liberalism as universal values. Writes American political scientist Samuel Huntington, "At a superficial level much of Western culture has indeed permeated the rest of the world. At a more basic level, however, Western concepts differ fundamentally from those prevalent in other civilizations. Western ideas of individualism, liberalism, constitutionalism, human rights, equality, liberty, the rule of law, democracy, free markets, the separation of church and state, often have little resonance in Islamic, Confucian, Japanese, Hindu, Buddhist or Othodox cultures."[6]

The attempt to universalize a practice often includes the urge to return to the original forms to dislodge cultural elements that have been appended over time, possibly changing or diverting the "pure" original teachings. For some American practitioners, it feels important to challenge the Asian cultural elements of Zen as irrelevant—but they may fail to realize that their practice can't help but be based on the worldview they've inherited from their own culture. American Sōtō Zen isn't and can't be a "pure" form of the practice washed clean of karmic conditioning and cultural influences. Even if somehow the Asian context can be left behind, that space is simply filled by the values and predispositions of the West.

Exposure to Zen practice can provide a startling and sometimes uncomfortable look at our assumptions about worldwide values. More than once I've heard a newly-arrived American practitioner in a Japanese training temple ask for handouts that explain the tasks of the various service positions. On learning that there are none, he or she frequently volunteers to create them, under the well-meaning but inaccurate assumption that the reason there are no handouts is that no one has ever thought of it before, or had the time or the skill to put them together. In fact, in a Japanese training temple we learn simply by observing and doing, not by reading explanations or asking why things are done in a particular way. This learning by wholehearted immersion is sometimes a shock to Americans, and their immediate response is to try to fix a system they perceive to be backward. As Huntington points out, "Western civilization is both Western and modern. Non-Western civilizations have attempted to become modern without becoming Western. To date only Japan has fully succeeded in this quest. Non-Western civilizations will continue to attempt to acquire the wealth, technology, skills, machines and weapons that are part of being modern. They will also attempt to reconcile this modernity with their traditional culture and values." [Huntington 49]

To me, precisely because Zen did not arise in a Western cultural context, it's a very effective opportunity to step back and look at our habituated thinking. Zen does not assume that suffering is abnormal and must be remedied at all costs. It does not assume that our value lies in those things for which we are publicly recognized. It does not assume that activity equals progress. It pulls us up short at every turn and challenges our expectations. *Is this or that idea really true? Or is it something I made up or inherited or took for granted? Is this really the only way to live? Or even the best way?*

Just as the fish can't see the water and the bird can't see the air, we are driven by cultural expectations that may remain invisible to us. These invisible expectations affect the way we receive and interpret the teachings. And yet, these expectations are not impurities that taint our vows. As bodhisattvas we vow to liberate numberless beings, end inexhaustible delusions, enter boundless dharma gates, and completely realize Buddha's unsurpassable awakening—and we give it everything we've got, including our misunderstandings and karmic hindrances. Clearly, these are not simple tasks that can be concretely manifested in the world of form, but that doesn't mean that our vows exist separate and unsullied somewhere in a higher plane. This One Unified Reality includes both delusion and awakening, both assumptions and insights, both the selfless aspiration of *bodhicitta* and the circumstances of the conditioned self. We can't separate a pure essence of Zen or vow or dharma from its conditioned cultural context. Whether or not a practitioner practices in a container that feels appropriate for him or her is another question. There is nothing wrong with considering whether or not any particular circumstance supports one's practice and awakening—as long as one remembers that there will always be a circumstance and that trying to look outside of it for an unspoiled essence won't help.

And, as always, when the problems of today's world seem insurmountable, we as bodhisattvas must take both the long view and small steps. I've been watching a BBC documentary series that follows the lives and work of four Church of England vicars in the rural diocese of Herefordshire. One, Father Matthew Cashmore, asks his parishioners to contribute produce from their gardens for the refugees stuck on the border in Calais and trying vainly to enter the country. The huge camps have been dismantled by the government and refugees are now without food, shelter, or other basic necessities. Father Matthew joins the volunteers delivering the truckload of food to Calais and preparing it for distribution, and is deeply moved by the experience, which stays with him for weeks afterward. I heard the voice of a bodhisattva when he described his effort to make sense of the work. "I'm coming to realize that all we can do is the good that's in front of us, the small good that's in front of us. I want my small bit to be an enormous bit. I want to be able to go over and fix it. But having an impatience for not being able to fix the big stuff is what drives you to do really big great stuff. So I'm going to carry on driving to fix the big stuff that I can't really fix, and I'm going to try and keep doing that and I'm going to keep failing and I'm going to keep falling on my face, but in the process of it I will get farther than if I just shrug my shoulders and go, 'Oh well, it's just too big a thing to deal with.'"[7]

I have frequently said in dharma talks that for a bodhisattva, Job One is not to look away. It's to simply show up, and keep showing up for our lives. Showing up means paying attention, looking for the large and small opportunities our modern Western lives give us to practice as bodhisattvas. Maybe our karmic conditions mean that we have significant physical resources to offer, and maybe we have only our aspiration and inspiration; either way, we have a real opportunity for some discernment about what skillful bodhisattva work really is. As a young self-made man, Andrew Carnegie, at one time the richest man in America, turned to Buddhism among other faith traditions in search of the answer to a deep personal question: *Why am I the one that's made all this money?* He went on to spend $350 million on philanthropy over the course of his life, perhaps in a continuing search for the answer. The average 21st-century bodhisattva is not working with causes and conditions—or resources—like these, and yet our efforts at relieving the suffering of the world and our questions about the best ways to do it in this day and age are equally valid.

As impermanent as they are, our karmic conditions are the ground of our practice, and there's nowhere else to go. They shape how we understand suffering, what we vow to do about it, and how we get that done. That means we need a real understanding of what we're offering and why. We are not offering an ancient Asian tradition to a modern West. We are offering the modern Western practice we've created from our ancestors' teachings because, given our karmic conditions and cultural filters, we can't offer anything else. As bodhisattvas, we can only offer ourselves.

NOTES

[1] McMahon, David. *The Making of Buddhist Modernism.* Oxford University Press, 2008, p. 5.

[2] Smith, Buster G. "American Buddhism: A Sociological Perspective." Dissertation, Baylor University, 2009.

[3] Irizarry, Joshua A. "Putting a Price on Zen: The Business of Redefining Religion for Global Consumption," *Journal of Global Buddhism* Vol. 16, 2015, p. 56.

[4] McMahon, p. 41.

[5] Sharf, Robert H. "Whose Zen? Zen Nationalism Revisited," *Rude Awakenings: Zen, the Kyoto School, and the Question of Nationalism* University of Hawai'i Press, 1995, p. 50

[6] Huntington, Samuel P. "The Clash of Civilizations?" *Foreign Affairs,* Vol. 72 No. 3, Summer 1993, p. 41

[7] "Episode 4." *A Vicar's Life.* British Broadcasting Corporation, 2018.

CHAPTER NINE
SHŌJU MAHLER

Opening the Door
in the West

When we receive the precepts, we take the bodhisattva vows and choose to follow this way of life having Shakyamuni Buddha, our dharma ancestors and our teachers as examples.

As Okumura Rōshi often says, "These are impossible and endless vows." But these vows are not ideas, a burden or an imposition. There are several ways to perceive "endless," and to me it conveys a sense of freedom. It signifies continuous practice and endless possibilities. It means that there is no pressure to achieve, to complete a study, a function or a task perfectly in a particular way and within a certain time period. "Endless" also means boundless in time and space. Our vows are boundless and they have consequences and repercussions, even though we are not aware of them, like an unheard echo.

There are numerous illustrations of our dharma ancestors, named or not, and we all are following the examples of teachers and practitioners, without them being aware of it at times. I have been extremely lucky to encounter guides who helped me on the path and who are still doing so through their teaching. Some were teachers, some novices, and some longtime practitioners but all these guides had a strong effect on me because they had left behind the mundane way of life.

Whether their culture supported them or they received the backing of their sangha or had to work at odd jobs to make their practice possible, they all had "left home" and chosen to follow the Buddhadharma.

So here I would like to acknowledge and thank them.

In the early days of my practice: Wade Hogetsu Hancock, my first non-teacher teacher who taught me how to do zazen and advised me to look for a teacher.

Joshin Bachoux Sensei of La Demeure sans Limites in France, the first Zen teacher I met.

My *tokudō* teacher Daien Bennage Rōshi, from whom I learned what practicing 24 hours a day means.

Shundo Aoyama Rōshi, Abbess of the Aichi Senmon Nisodo in Nagoya, Japan. Even though I do not understand Japanese, she taught me greatly just by her physical presence.

The Venerable Thich Nhat Hanh, who helped me understand Shakyamuni Buddha's teachings in a very pragmatic way.

My longtime unwavering and supportive dharma friend Reverend Jokei Lambert, now abbess of La Demeure sans Limites.

Reverend Issho Fujita and Reverend Taiken Yokoyama, both of whom heard me and gave me advice at a point in my practice when I was having a very difficult time.

And especially, with deep gratitude, my teacher Okumura Rōshi, who opened the door wide and, constantly supportive, teaching patiently and steadfastly, lets everyone practice, learn, and advance on the path at his or her own pace.

Before I met Okumura Rōshi, his own teacher, Kōshō Uchiyama Rōshi, unbeknownst to him, had an impact on my life. When I was practicing as a lay person at the Bear Tree Zendo in New Hampshire and it was my turn to be tenzo, the priest told me to read Uchiyama Rōshi's book *Refining your Life.* In it Uchiyama Rōshi says, "When you are born, your entire world is born with you, and when you die, so dies your entire world." I had no idea who Uchiyama Rōshi was, but this teaching accompanies me to this day, through his voice as well as Shakyamuni Buddha's in the *Dhammapada*:

We are what we think.
All that we are arises with our thoughts.
With our thoughts we make the world.[1]

I do not know the name of the monk who nearly twenty-five years ago now, in a Zen center in California, showed me the practice of *gyōhatsu*, eating using ōryōki. As he wrapped the bowls, placing the corner of the cloth away from him, he said, "We give," and then bringing the other end towards him he continued, "and we receive." It was a shock as I perceived what he meant, and at the same time it was a huge question mark. This monk did not know that giving and receiving would be a leading thread through my practice.

The other crucial teaching I received as a novice is when I heard Okumura Rōshi give a dharma talk about the Zen monk Ryōkan and his poem "Butterfly Dreams":

With no mind the flower invites the butterfly,
With no mind the butterfly visits the flower.
When the flower opens, the butterfly comes,
When the butterfly comes, the flower opens.
I am the same, I do not know other people

And they do not know me.
But without knowing one another,
We naturally follow the universal law.

Ryōkan lived alone, supporting himself by doing *takuhatsu*, and it is said that he had no disciples, but he is much admired and naturally, through his example and his poems, he does have many followers.

My personal vow stems from the example of all these teachers, whether I met them or not, but most of all from the practice of my teacher, Okumura Rōshi.

My vow is to give back what I have received by making available a place in France where people can come practice zazen in the Sōtō Zen tradition and study the Dharma.

I have also wanted to translate Buddhist works from English to French, as there is much written in English, and now I am focusing on translating some of Uchiyama Rōshi's and Okumura Rōshi's teachings.

If Shakyamuni Buddha said the dharma could be taught in one's own dialect, it stems from this principle that the outward form of the practice will be influenced by the culture of this different language. Buddhism has always accepted and included outward forms of the different places to which it travelled. This certainly can be observed in countries as different as Sri Lanka and China, for example. But the fundamental teachings of the dharma, though they are seen from different perspectives, have not deviated from the Buddha's basic teachings.

In what way can form evolve in the West to meet people's needs, without the fundamental teachings of Buddhism being either distorted or only superficially transmitted? Changed into a "feel good" practice or taken over and transformed by Western psychology? Or who knows what else? I think this is and will continue to be a core issue in the 21st century until the dharma is deeply rooted here.

I have no answer to this question. It has only been 60 years since Sōtō Zen has been adopted and practiced by non-Buddhist Westerners in the United States and 50 years in Europe. And now one hears much talk of "new branches," when younger Western teachers become successors in the Sōtō Zen communities. And yes, it is wonderful that there are offshoots. But what of roots? Deep, broad, strong roots to steady and nourish the young tree of the dharma in the West?

This is essential and my vow is to show practitioners that it is crucial to help profoundly anchor the tree in European soil right where they are. There are numerous ways the dharma can permeate a culture, and I would like my students to understand what it means to practice as a community and to know that all people have their own difficulties and strong points. We need to support each other and practice in harmony while walking on the path. So I would like my students to perceive deeply that the sangha is everywhere, is everything they meet.

I would like them to know that nothing and no one is either superior or inferior, as they live and actualize the dharma in their own personal ways.

Today, we want to obtain what we want right away, so quickly, in fact, that some people say that everything is changing too quickly. Can we have the humility and the wisdom to accept that Buddhism is in its infancy in the West? Can we have the patience to keep sitting, practicing and studying profoundly for the long term? To have, in Shunryu Suzuki Rōshi's expression, "beginner's mind" for many, many more years?

Once several years ago Okumura Rōshi was giving a dharma talk and spoke about a teaching I had neither read about nor heard of. I am sorry I cannot remember what it was, but when I asked him if it existed in English he said, with a half-smile, "Not yet." It was as if I got hit in the stomach, as I understood it as meaning that it is here in time and space but has not yet appeared in the West. So we need to be patient and practice, and at the same time not be dogmatic, not construct an imagined new belief system in a new land. We need to be flexible and patient like the sprig of lily of the valley I once saw slowly unfurling its leaves and blooming through a tarred driveway.

Ksanti, patience, one of the paramitas, is also sometimes translated as forebearance, which is not, in my view, the correct way for a bodhisattva to perceive or practice *ksanti*. Forebearance can have the meaning of tolerance, fortitude, or endurance, and I understand this as implying a sense of superiority that creates a considerable separation between ourselves and all other beings.

I prefer to think of patience as openness, a wide, long, and deep view. Once Okumura Rōshi said to me, "A teacher is someone who opens the door." He did not say that the teacher makes it difficult to go through the door, that we have to hurry through the door, or that there is only one way to perceive going through the door. If the teacher does nothing but open the door wide and keep walking on the path, then there are endless possibilities of practice for the student, according to her or his aptitudes and inclinations. Therefore there are numberless ways the dharma can permeate the culture and embrace it and its people.

To embrace, a word that came from Greek, went to Latin, into French and then English, means "to clasp in the arms." When we take someone in our arms or include something in our life, we at the same time are embraced. There is this matter-of-course giving and receiving from everything in Indra's net. As we wholly sit and practice in the new land, in the new culture, without forcing anything, the dharma slowly embraces and is embraced by the new soil.

A few months ago a new mailman came to deliver a package at my temple in France and, not saying a word, put his hands in *gasshō* before leaving. Recently in an airport a man ran up to me and asked if I was a Zen Buddhist priest and we talked. I got on the plane and the young woman sitting next to me was reading the *Dhammapada*.

The Western soil is slowly being planted with the seeds of the dharma, and they need to be watered attentively and responsibly for numerous generations until naturally they sprout and mature.

We are so lucky that the conditions are here for us to receive the dharma from the teachers who brought us Shakyamuni Buddha's and Dōgen Zenji's teachings. It is our practice as second- or third-generation practitionners to make sure that it is passed on correctly and as deeply as we possibly can. In order to be able to do that, we need to keep practicing, doing zazen and studying the dharma.

Again and again we have to let go of our fixed views and we have to stop having an automatic negative reaction to different perspectives, old or new ways of practicing, of embodying and spreading the dharma. It is difficult to be open to change.

The first time I went to practice in Japan at an *ango* at the Aichi Senmon Nisōdō, the nun who was showing me around the temple and who spoke some English said, "Here we practice the Nisōdō way." It meant "Leave at the gate everything you have been taught." It was very difficult but a great teaching for me, right from the start. When leaving our fixed views at the gate is possible, then everything is open, and all beings are alive together.

Realizing this is *prajñā*, the wisdom to see deeply, to see things as they are. All the paramitas—*dana* (giving), *sila* (precepts), *ksanti* (patience), *virya* (diligence or energy) and *dhyana* (meditation or zazen)—contain each other, and they all include and are included in *prajñā*. Without *prajñā* they are not paramitas.

When we wake up to the reality of all beings, when we know that without everything and everyone else we cannot live, naturally we support all beings. Like Avalokiteshvara who has the eye of wisdom in each of her/his thousands of hands of action, we are no longer afraid, no longer strangers to life. Avalokiteshvara can manifest in any form, at any time; what helps each one of us is different. Like him/her, and as the ancestors and our teachers have done before us, we in the 21st century need to look profoundly. We need to just be, and use a thousand tools with understanding and compassion for all beings, including ourselves.

NOTES

[1] Byrom, Thomas. *Dhammapada: The Sayings of the Buddha.* Shambala, 1993, p. xv.

[2] Okumura, Shohaku. "The 28th Chapter of *Shōbōgenzō: Bodaisatta-Shishobō." Dharma Eye* No. 14, August 2004.

The Bodhisattva Heart

I firmly believe that the heart of the world is a bodhisattva heart. I believe that we find bodhisattvas in the three times and in the ten thousand directions as well as in every spiritual and religious tradition. I believe that bodhisattvas quietly and serenely, and maybe some others times more noisily, all according to their lives, culture, time, and causes and conditions, have worked, are working and will continue to work for the sake of all existences beyond space and time into infinity. I believe that the whole universe, the infinitesimal one as well as the macrocosmic one not yet discovered, pulsates with the heart of all bodhisattvas. That is how strong and boundless this faith is ingrained in my body/mind, one with the five skandhas allowing me to feel, think, and share this wonderful path in this life given by wondrous karma.

The truth is that this faith and profound feeling are beyond words, but words are as well precious instruments, useful because they allow us to share and find common ground in our life in community.

Without words, how could we have been reached and touched by the teachings and examples of Shakyamuni Buddha, Dōgen Zenji and all the ancestors who have transmitted the light of dharma through words and writings?

I think and feel that when we enter this path—and I am not sure if we really know when it starts for each one of us (no-beginning and no-end)—the practice and listening to the teachings can present difficulties, and maybe we have a naïve way of comprehending them. The heart too needs to be trained. Being a bodhisattva is not only wanting to do good and putting others first; it requires as well learning little by little, experience after experience, teacher after teacher, how to, where to, and when to do good—or, simply put, how and when to act appropriately for the benefit of others as our main motivation. As Avalokitesvara has a hand for everyone and for every circumstance, the bodhisattva with all his heart and body needs to experience and learn when to talk, act or remain quiet and do nothing, if this is for the benefit of all beings. As bodhisattvas, we walk and awake in this path. One step at a time, we move in *kinhin* in an infinite circle, following the steps of Buddha and ancestors for kalpas without end.

BODHISATTVAS OF THE 21ST CENTURY

Who are they? Where are they? What are they doing that makes them different (or not) from others? Bodhisattvas are like any other human being, or beings. They live this life with the chores that each one has to carry on in society as part of his or her commitment and practice: spouses, mothers, fathers, grandfathers, teachers, doctors, lawyers, monks and nuns, priest and welders, mechanics and garbage collectors, animal trainers and veterinarians. As bodhisattvas, they have in common the heart that wants to give it all to help all beings walk a path of light, realization, and true happiness, regardless of spiritual tradition or lack thereof, not only for those who consider themselves or want to be Buddhist.

Bodhisattvas, although living in the ordinary world and accomplishing ordinary things in everyday life, live a life that is led by the vow of awakening through practice on the cushion and in each day's activity, all of it for the sake of all beings. Loving parents, no matter what they may be doing or planning, have in mind always the best interest of their children; they live pulled by the noble desire of offering the best opportunities to their offspring. Bodhisattvas also have the best interest of all beings in their hearts, but they are pulled by vow rather than by karma. They have made a choice to live a life that takes into account the spiritual well-being of the world, detaching themselves from any personal interest; they have a commitment to listen with their hearts to the cries of the world and transform it in awakening by offering healing words, actions, harmony of view and a life that includes the joys and sorrows of all beings.

The bodhisattva life is one of never-ending transformation. Life is by nature impermanent. How can we remain the same (same views, same opinions, same strategies and actions) if everything around us is always changing? To be born, grow older, get sick and die are the major changes we, if fortunate, will get to see coming into our lives. But in between, all the colors of the rainbow, the gay ones and the sad ones, the joyful ones and the dramatic ones, will color our lives and all existences included in them in unimaginable ways. Bodhisattvas, pulled by vow, welcome those changes—little ones, subtle ones, striking ones. Naked to the wind, arms open, and head to the sky, they cry or rejoice but overall embrace those changes over which they have no power. The only understanding is that bodhisattvas allow themselves again and again, time and time again, to flow into the transformation that comes their way with everything that happens.

THE FOUR VOWS

These are the leading vows of bodhisattvas of all times, from beginningless times to endless times. We read and study them; we ponder and wonder about them. We try to apply them in our lives through the study and life experience of the precepts, the four noble truths and the examples of our ancestors. We fail, we start again and again; we lose courage for a moment; we repent of our wrong deeds and defilements every time we sit on the cushion. Finally one day we wake up to the understanding that our practice is without aim or gain, without limit and or a place to go or end. We have to keep coming back to our resolve, to the cushion, to the bodhisattva vows and to our own personal vow in this our lifetime, without dismay. A bodhisattva knows that if our hearts want to follow the steps of Buddha and ancestors, we need to keep accepting our humanity and karma, balancing it with our vow to keep awakening for the sake of the world. We need to trust that we are supported in every way by Buddhas and ancestors of the past, present, and future. Our ancestors count on us, on our life and practice, to become alive and keep those wondrous teachings flowing within the ocean of this existence and all existences in samsara/nirvana, life/death, and this and all infinite universes past, present, and to come.

These general vows, as well as the very specific ones we have embraced and committed to follow, are deeply ingrained in our cells and DNA, so to speak. Our transformation from a heart of a bodhisattva to a life of one changes our body/mind. I do not know how; I can only attest to the strength of this conviction and to its reality for me. This statement expresses my trust in the support of ancestors, not only of the Soto Zen tradition that I have chosen to carry on and share with my life, but of the bodhisattvas (call them saints, prophets, messiahs, or any other name according to the diverse traditions) and ancestors of all traditions. I have faith as well that our karma, with our practice, keeps making space for more wisdom and availability for us to realize what needs to be realized in every aspect of life. But we know karma is being created all the time as long as we are alive and talking, thinking, acting, and having desires, no matter how noble they may be. That transformation of body/mind, which happens gradually as well as suddenly all through our existence, happens as we bring our life to the cushion during zazen, opening the hand of thought, as Kosho Uchiyama Rōshi used to say, and when we take our practice from the cushion to our daily life, letting and allowing anything to come and go during all the hours and events of the days, weeks, months, and years.

Like my teacher, Okumura Rōshi, I deeply believe that zazen, our silent and unmovable practice, is the center and foundation of our bodhisattva life. Without it, any other expression of our bodhisattva being is empty, just a collection of void words or actions, like an eggshell with no substance. Zazen, like the center of a bicycle wheel, sustains, supports, and radiates in every direction of the circle of our lives and beyond toward infinity. Nothing is left untouched or unchanged from this foundational experience when it is real and sincere practice. We do not need to know how this change operates. We need to experience and see it in our lives and in the lives of those who are touched by our lives, which are no longer our personal ego-centered lives, but the life of dharma flowing through us.

TEACHERS OF THE PATH OPEN DOORS TO THE INFINITE DHARMA

When I met my teacher, I had been without a teacher for awhile. I was practicing with a zazen group I had started in Miami and then in Delray Beach, Florida. I wanted to support my own practice and share the treasure of what a sangha is, which for me has been the expression and vessel of all Three Treasures. However, I was in limbo because a teacher was a very important part of my practice and of the Three Treasures. I had for some years a wonderful teacher in Venezuela, a French disciple of Taisen Deshimaru Rōshi. He was my first teacher, Yves Zengaku Nansen Carouget (1926-2010), who opened my life to the practice at a time when I had lost ground due to the tragic death of my partner. I did not know what life was about anymore; all my certainties, which were many and as strong as my will, had been blown away in a few seconds. I was left emotionally and spiritually frail and shattered.

I started practice some months after that tragic loss. I had no idea what Zen or zazen was. Sitting in front of a wall quietly, tears rolling down my cheeks, no one telling me it was going to get better, I allowed my life, as it was, to unfold and to figure out whatever needed to be figured out. All of it was simply a deep calming experience, although I didn't know how or why. Three years later, as I was going to France, my teacher suggested I participate in *jukai*. I did not hesitate, but just felt the need to do what he was suggesting. I stitched together the pieces of my rakusu in five days at La Gendronnière, the temple founded during Deshimaru Rōshi's lifetime and then and now managed by his several disciples. Tears again were rolling down my cheeks, and then everything came together. I knew then and there that I wanted to follow this path even if I still had so much to learn. It was a very important moment. The rakusu gave me strength and resolve to move forward, still in the middle of not knowing where this was leading to. By then I had partially abandoned the pressing need I had to live making "clear" decisions about my life. I was still living this letting go of control as a loss since I had always made decisions about my direction. My will had led my life.

Then my second teacher, Roland Yuno Rech, another disciple of Deshimaru, crossed my path. I was living in Paris, France. His soft manners and approach to the practice opened another dharma door. The dharma was manifesting itself in diverse ways. I undertook *shukke tokudō* (novice ordination) under his guidance in 1995. Changing countries in a short period of time created a vacuum for a while, but the practice was always there. Then I decided to go to a monastery with Jean-Pierre Taiun Faure, again another disciple of Taisen Deshimaru Rōshi. I made a commitment to sell the little house I had just recently bought in Florida in my confusion about where to live and what to do, but I got stuck in the United States because of the national financial crisis of the time. In that year I went to meet Okumura Rōshi, looking for a teacher to practice with while waiting to go back to France. Without knowing it yet, I had come to the end of my spiritual search for a teacher. In that year I visited Sanshin several times, still thinking I was waiting for the moment to go to the monastery in France. I remember saying to Okumura Rōshi in one of our first interviews that I knew what I wanted to do: go to France, to a monastery with Jean-Pierre Taiun. He replied: "I am glad you know what you want." His calm answer has remained a koan in my life. Did he say so knowing I was in a delusional state of mind, or was he just being a mirror of my own desires? I can say now that I was really looking for a teacher but did not have much clarity about it. Every time I went to Sanshin to a Genzō-e (retreat focusing on study of Dōgen's *Shōbōgenzō*), I would have tears flowing naturally during the teachings, no drama about it. The only thing I could comprehend was that for the very first time someone was speaking a language that seemed so right, familiar and straight to my bones and heart, rather than to my intellectual brain. I was having diarrhea too, and I was not sick with any physical ailment. It was the illness of my life being healed by the touch of the true dharma flowing from all the kalpas through the teachings of Okumura Rōshi and entering my own body. It affected my body/mind in a very physical way. At that time and still not understanding he was the teacher I had been searching for even before my birth (my strong ego was getting in the way), I told him what was happening to me: tears and diarrhea. He apologized, and vibrantly I was able to say to him: "Please don't. It is not your fault in any way. It is the dharma that you allow to come forward through your body, mind, and speech and that transforms something in me." I added, "Like the rays of light in the stained glass windows of a cathedral, light comes through you and illuminates everything that it touches." However, at that time and moment, I still had not realized he was the teacher I needed and wanted.

A year went by and one day—I clearly remember it—in the early morning I suddenly woke up, in every sense of the word. I knew there and then that Okumura Rōshi was the teacher for whom I had been searching. My first reaction was one of dismay: my true teacher was in the United States and I wanted to go to France! There was a confrontation between what I—my ego-centered view—had planned for so long and what the dharma was bringing into my life as a realization. I put all that aside and called Sanshin immediately to speak with Okumura Rōshi and ask him if he would accept me as his disciple. He listened and asked me if I was certain about this. I told him there were no doubts about it. He asked me to write to each one of my previous teachers to communicate what I had decided. It took me months to write those three letters, since I owed so much to each one of them and wanted to explain how they had, in their infinite generosity, walked me to this moment of my life. I wanted to be loving and caring and try to convey how there was no choice being made here about who is the best teacher, but just a continuation of a path lead by karma and dharma, which had guided me to this place and time to share with Okumura Rōshi as my teacher.

After that very foundational moment, I understood that we do not choose a teacher because the location is convenient or from any other rational or mundane logic. If our practice is sincere, I believe, the dharma manifesting itself in every way and at every moment will put forward what you need to realize. It may be gradually or, as in my case, suddenly, although I am sure that that year of coming to Sanshin prepared me for what awakened that early Monday morning. Writing those letters at that time to each one of my previous teachers, I experienced how difficult and painful it can be to change from one teacher or lineage to another, even if one is absolutely clear about what direction to take. I have been able to ponder it and share with others going through it, including one of my disciples. My conclusion is that we do not owe fidelity to anyone other than to the dharma, wherever and however it may guide us in our path. We do not abandon a teacher or a lineage or a sangha; teachers, sanghas and lineages are dharma doors we enter for the sake of all beings. When we make a change to be under the guidance of another teacher, we deeply bow in unending gratitude to the teacher, sangha, and dharma that has until then supported our practice and led us to where we are headed now. There should be no guilt, blame, or regrets of any sort; ultimately we are just walking the infinite path of our life with the guidance of the life and light of the dharma. Every true teacher understands this.

In another related consideration, I believe that when we make a move such as changing to a new teacher or lineage, we all learn: the person making that move, as well as the teacher and sangha to whom we are saying farewell. It allows us all to ask questions: why is the person changing directions? Something we did or did not do? It would be a wonderful teaching and learning moment for all if that person could have the opportunity to say "So long!" and bow in gratitude to everyone, explaining his/her reasons and not feeling rejected or being looked upon as a traitor. Unfortunately, I have seen negative reactions happen more than once, making it more painful and confusing for everyone.

My Personal Vows

It took some time and life experience to be able to see and understand what was presenting itself as a life mission, which became my vows. As my teacher was following his teacher's vows, I had him as a great inspiration through his life and daily dedication for years embodying this path. Ultimately, I was able to clarify what I wanted and needed to do to embrace a work of love for all beings. I wanted with all my heart and life to share this path with others, Buddhists or not, and to help make Okumura Rōshi's understanding of our tradition more widely available. One of those vows has been to translate Zen texts from French and English into Spanish. I had translated Zen texts before with my two previous teachers, so somehow there was already a direction, although at that point it was not yet a vow. A sense of urgency arose. I really wanted others to have access to these wonderful teachings, so I started translating some of Okumura Rōshi's texts with his permission. I have to confess, I have been slow to accomplish what I had set as a mission. I ask forgiveness for this. I have translated two texts so far, *Introduction to Zen* and *The Wholehearted Way*. Other books are waiting in line. Unfortunately, it has been difficult for me and my dharma brother Denshō Quintero in Colombia to find someone in the Hispanic publishing world who is interested in this type of work. I am not dismayed because I know I have no control over this but need to trust the great dharma ways to guide us when the time becomes right. Other books have been lined up for translation: Dōgen Zenji's waka poems[5] and *Living by Vow*. I hope to have the energy and the causes and conditions to accomplish this much-needed work to reach sanghas in the Hispanic world.

As an extension of this vow, I have encouraged my disciples in Germany and in Venezuela to study and translate my teacher's texts. My German disciple Ryōshun Lutz has already translated *Living by Vow*, which has been accepted for publication in Germany by an important publishing house specializing in spiritual and religious books. It had already published Okumura Rōshi's *Genjōkōan*. The German sangha and I are extremely happy that this can happen, as it helps to spread his unique and deep understanding of the teachings. On the other hand, it allows the sangha I guide spiritually to base our work on the practice and study of this precious material, which has become essential for our understanding of the teachings in our tradition and lineage. For his consistent and tireless efforts, we are and will always be unconditionally grateful to Okumura Rōshi's life and dedication to the translation of Dōgen's work.

My second vow—and maybe the one to which I have applied myself even more since I started walking this path in 1987—has been to share the practice of zazen. Wherever I have been living—Venezuela, France, Germany, and the United States—I have always started a zazen group. Many times I was asked to add the study of texts, but at each opportunity I felt that there was a lot of material around, like books, audio recordings, or YouTube videos, but not enough time dedicated to silence and practice. I was then and am now convinced that although it's important to study, the texts won't make much sense if one has not yet established the practice of zazen as a foundation of this path and one's life. Following my teacher's example with determination, I try my best to share the absolute foundation of the practice of zazen, insisting that it is very important to practice intensely, and not only a little once in a while, in order to break the ceiling of ignorance that crushes us. It is so unfortunate to see how people just toy with the practice without thinking, as they try very hard to accommodate the practice to their own personal needs, understanding, and convenience. Instead of the Sanshin style of sitting for fifty-minute periods, they want to do only twenty or thirty minutes. We can hear all types of reasoning. A lack of trust, understanding, and experience precents people from going beyond a certain point in their practice. As I repeat so many times, our practice is a real treasure; it will not open up to us deeply if we do not try harder and with determination to find the path that leads to the enjoyment of this treasure. Practice becomes a twenty-minute sitting that satisfies one's conscience and provides a sense that one is doing something spiritually good. This type of practice, I believe, does not change our life; we can go on for years doing it this way, unable to break the ceiling of our ignorance. Nevertheless, I have come to understand that maybe this is the way it is for many, according to their causes and conditions, karma and circumstances, and it may be better to belong to a sangha than to a golf or poker club. We will all be transformed by the teachings and go from darkness and ignorance into realization, but we have to trust that there is a way and time for each one of us. So I let go of any judgments and accept that people are where they are. I continue to help others to sit fifty minutes and overcome their own fear and mental limitations about their bodies and the practice. It has become a vow.

My third vow has become one of everyday presence in my life. I wake up, live, and go to bed with it in body and mind. It has to do with my body. As a result of a very bad radiation treatment for cancer in 1992, over the last six years I have seen a progressive but clear decline in my walking. The nerves in my hips are not sending the necessary signals to my legs to do what we do to walk without having to think about it. I now have to walk with a cane and cannot do so without looking, thinking, and considering every step or turn I take. Here and now, practice has taken over the 24/7 of daily life. How I move, breathe, sit, get up, and make any other physical move-ment involves my entire being. The vow has been to make of this circumstance a deep opportunity for the practices of patience, love, and learning. I do not fight what is happening. I adjust to it every day as I continue to live and share life with others. I make the most of it. I have gained a deeper capacity to listen to others, to share the joy of living, and to develop other abilities I would never have cultivated without slowing down. As I work in the hospice field with terminally ill and dying patients, I can see how much life is still in me to support their journey and to better understand with my own body and experience what it is to progressively leave behind the body and life you knew before. When we quiet and slow down, we can hear the whispers of the world; when people are dying they still have so much life to share in a minute that the sense of time takes on another meaning and dimension.

I am profoundly grateful for my life. The path I've taken starting at a very young age has made me work with my body. I was a dancer, a good one; I learned to submit my body to the desires of overcoming gravity and push it to extremes to widen the range of movements and body language. As I encountered Zen practice, the body started going in the other direction: sit down quietly and do not move. Breathe. But it was still a body practice. Then came the progression of muscle stiffness, and I had to learn to move in other ways and consider other aspects. My practice deepened and entered into every dimension of my life. Sitting became natural and fortunately not a problem at all. It is as if now sitting can happen for hours, and to paraphrase my teacher, what a treat to just sit with nothing to do or think and no place to go.

In the autumn of my life, sitting with all my heart, body and mind as one has become a precious gift, a treasure that took its time to uncover itself fully, although life may still reserve surprises for the path, since everything is impermanent. But overall, the vow to practice and to share zazen and everything that springs from that central and foundational practice, is the vow that today my body/mind lives and expresses joyfully and deeply. My gratitude is infinite to my teachers, spiritual ancestors, parents, karma, causes and conditions, as well as my illness and its healing in my life. I can only repay my debt by giving my whole being to this life of dharma for the benefit of all beings in the three times and the ten thousand directions.

CHAPTER ELEVEN

JŌKEI WHITEHEAD

Each Thing is Everything

WE CAST A SHADOW ON SOMETHING WHEREVER WE STAND, AND IT IS NO GOOD MOVING FROM PLACE TO PLACE TO SAVE THINGS.... CHOOSE A PLACE WHERE YOU WON'T DO VERY MUCH HARM AND STAND IN IT FOR ALL YOU ARE WORTH, FACING THE SUNSHINE.

— E.M. FORSTER

Bodhisattvas, or people who consider themselves such, can be annoying. A vow is not an identity ripe for reification; it's an awareness, a commitment, and a reminder of how often we miss the mark. As with the Dharma in *Genjōkōan*, if we think we have it, we're far away.

I'm picturing the chalkboard in high school math, where my teacher has drawn a curve that approaches infinitely closer to an axis without ever touching it. We might feel failure because we never attain our aspiration. But if a vow has guided the entire trajectory of our lives, we can't say it didn't do anything.

Before immersing myself full-time in Zen practice, I lived in Japan for five years, studying Buddhism on my own and visiting temples every vacation. The private language school where I taught English suffered from conflict between its sales and teaching staff. The final step in recruiting new students was an oral test to assess their English. These "level checks" were the first time prospective students met a teacher rather than a salesperson. Some students decided not to join the school after this experience, which the salespeople blamed on the teachers. For their part, many teachers regarded the sales staff as sleazy operators who would say anything to sign new students and made a pile of money doing so. It seemed likely to me that racial and class bias played a role in the hostility: almost all the sales staff were from India and Pakistan, while the teachers were all white and mostly from the UK.

After a few years of teaching, I was offered a promotion to manage a video learning program. I wasn't interested in distance learning, so I asked about another new position: managing the relationship between sales and teaching. My boss tried to dissuade me. "There's a lot of bad feeling; both sides will hate you." But to me it was an intriguing challenge—was there a way to redeem longstanding mistrust and resentment between two groups?

I already knew how the teachers thought and behaved because I was one. But I knew nothing about the salespeople's work, so I met with their manager and asked a lot of questions, focusing on quantifiable facts: How many cold calls to find one interested person? How many hours spent with a prospective student before they came in for a level check? How are salespeople paid? The manager was surprised by my curiosity, but to me it seemed essential. How could I mediate between two sides if I understood only one?

Given the data, it was clear to me that the fundamental problem was the teachers' ignorance of the salespeople's job and pay structure, and also of how it felt to prospective students to be grilled in a foreign language. We needed education to replace the assumptions and prejudices.

I met with teachers in small groups, posing the same questions I asked the sales manager and having them guess the answers. How many calls for one meeting? How many hours to land one level check? What was a salesperson's average pay? I wrote their guesses on a whiteboard. Next to them I wrote a second column of numbers, the real ones from the sales manager. I pointed to the space between the columns and said, "This is our problem." The truth itself did the work of changing the teachers' attitudes: the simple facts of what it was like to be someone else, to do the job they did.

On the testing front, because of the overarching power imbalance between student and teacher, we needed something other than facts and figures; we teachers needed the emotional experience of being quizzed in a foreign language by an intimidating authority figure. I prevailed upon the Japanese head of the school, whom we knew only by fearsome reputation, to administer the level check in Japanese to each of us. Some teachers had lived in Japan for awhile and were quite fluent, others not at all. Their grade on the test didn't matter for their jobs, just as it didn't really matter which English level a new student was assigned—it was the feeling of the interaction, the proportion of fun to fear, that left the impression.

At that time I knew nothing of the twelve links of causation (ignorance being the first), and I didn't know much about the bodhisattva vows. But based on my Buddhist reading, I hoped that giving people the chance to experience a situation from another person's perspective would change the way they inhabited their own. And these experiments succeeded. Teachers and salespeople began working together; some became friends. The number of prospective students fleeing the school in shame or frustration after their level checks declined. To me this was tangible proof that Buddhism worked, that practicing oneness could change the world.

The central vow I took at ordination was the bodhisattva vow to save all beings. Okumura Rōshi has said that saving all beings means being one with all beings. This understanding has been vital for me, because people sometimes like to idealize priests and elevate practice centers above "the real world." Yet such separations contradict the bodhisattva vow.

When I arrived at Tassajara Zen Mountain Center in 2005 to begin my formal training, I was struck by how often students referred to *in here* and *out there*, as in, "People are so much nicer in here than out there." I had no idea what they were talking about. The practitioners at Tassajara seemed to me much like people anywhere—fully human, endowed with both "thief nature and Buddha nature," as Kodo Sawaki Rōshi noted. Since I had recently immigrated from *out there*, I would surely have noticed a substantial difference in niceness. What I saw instead was this discrimination.

Would a bodhisattva see herself as a bodhisattva, which necessarily means seeing some others as not-bodhisattvas? Would a bodhisattva think in such dualistic terms? Would she elevate herself above others?

We're taught the image of the bodhisattva helping people across the river separating samsara from nirvana. And yet these two shores are one land, as Dōgen tells us over and over in his dazzling displays of poetry and paradox, all based on one truth: each thing is everything. Practice is enlightenment. Delusion and enlightenment are interdependent, woven together to make Buddha's robe. Samsara and nirvana suffuse each other. Our difficulty is in perceiving them within each other, like Okumura Rōshi's picture of the old and young woman. When we're in samsara, nirvana feels as if it doesn't exist. And in nirvana, samsara doesn't matter. Sickness and health, life and death, so many things feel like this.

The bodhisattva's task is not only to find the oneness, the unity of form and emptiness, of difference and sameness, but to *be* this oneness, to manifest the equality of all things as reminder and inspiration. This is "so-called enlightenment": being and acting in harmony with all things. Seeing the world whole, living it whole, and loving it whole—"joyful participation in a world of sorrows," in the words of Pico Iyer. Standing for all you're worth, facing the sunshine, because bodhisattvas need joy as much as determination.

I think some people naturally do this, without needing any particular resolution. Others have to spell it out, to say, "This is what I'm devoting my life to." And then spend every day thereafter trying to figure out what we've promised, and what our promise means in each moment. I don't think it means always being nice and giving people what they want, or never saying no. If you can't say no, then your yes is meaningless. The bodhisattva no is important.

I first learned about religions other than Christianity and Judaism when I was about twelve. My history teacher said that Shintō holds that everything in the world has a spirit, even things we don't consider alive. I looked down at my desk, initials carved on top and gum fermenting underneath, with newfound curiosity and respect. I have no memory of Dr. Pisani's descriptions of Buddhism, Taoism, Hinduism, or Islam, but I've never forgotten that moment of wonder, the possibility that everything I'd ever taken for granted might in fact be party to a mysterious sacredness secretly shared by all things.

Partly thanks to that moment, I've believed fiercely in the equality of all people and things since childhood. This conviction has held its own despite our society's pervasive brainwashing, both obvious and subtle, telling us that certain races, genders, and classes of people are more valuable than others. And that human beings matter more than other living and non-living things.

These discriminations result in devastating inequities in people's access to necessities, opportunities for fulfillment, health, safety, and freedom. On a wider scale, privileging human beings above all other life and non-life wreaks havoc on our planet, our home—the ultimate no-win situation. Each thing is everything.

The first time I saw Okumura Rōshi, a decade ago, what caught my attention was something absent—the attitude that seemed to emanate from some brown robes, a whiff of "Here Comes The Teacher." Okumura Rōshi's entrance into the Buddha Hall was empty of that, as was his way of speaking. And yet during his dharma talk, I finally understood several things that had eluded me until then.

Although I found my teacher that day, and with him, a Dharma I could engage in a challenging and meaningful way, I still had to navigate the hierarchies and personality clashes of temple life, the ways in which *in here* was not better than *out there*, no matter how we tried to make it so.

When I sat *tangaryō* at Tassajara, there were only five of us, sitting in a row. After a few days, my knees were feeling the pain, and I considered moving to a chair. But no one had done that yet, and I didn't want to be the first to "crack." Then I asked myself what kind of person I wanted to be—one who willfully harmed her body to feed her ego, or who took care of herself in an appropriate way? I moved to a chair, then back to the cushion. Others did the same. And I vowed never again to try to use my practice to impress anyone.

This vow became my touchstone in working with a teacher I deeply respect, and whom many people put on a pedestal. It's often taken for granted within Zen communities that we should idealize teachers; this conviction could be considered the first rule of temple hierarchy.

Okumura Rōshi never requested such treatment, but that didn't stop people from offering it. And those who offered it most zealously were frequently the same ones who treated their fellow practitioners with arrogance. Which makes perfect sense. If I subscribe to a system of inequality that requires me to elevate someone above myself, then I will naturally believe in my right under that system to elevate myself above others; it's logical. Yet the bodhisattva vow asks us to renounce such cherished human hierarchies, the pedestals and put-downs, because saving all beings means being one with all beings.

Before moving to Bloomington, I queried several people who had practiced at Sanshinji to find out what it was like. One advised, "People who don't stand up for themselves can get bullied." To some this might seem an appalling thing to hear about a Zen temple, but to me it sounded like the world as we know it—no *in here* or *out there*.

The first time I arrived home from morning practice hopping mad was because the very person who had warned me about bullying had turned around and tried a little on me, no doubt unconsciously and also unsuccessfully. A tug-of-war requires two people, and I refused to join. Because as soon as a second person picks up the rope of struggle, someone will win and someone will lose, and both are responsible for wreaking this inequity, often over a prize worth nothing, like what we think other people think of us. If I allow myself to be bullied, then I'm letting someone else be a bully, and doing no one any karmic favors. It's not losing that's wrong; it's the game.

Despite such occasional karmic drama, I respected the priests I practiced with at Sanshinji. But I found temple life more enjoyable when the sangha became more diverse as more laypeople joined. I was happy when we got some fresh air, some real beginner's mind—people who didn't assume they knew the one right way to do things or feel responsible for enlightening everyone else.

In fairness, being a Zen priest is a tough gig. Just before I left Japan, I visited Eiheiji with a friend. There I met a Japanese priest I really liked and respected. I asked him if he'd ever been to Tassajara, and what he thought of it. He hesitated as people do when they don't want to say anything negative. I assured him that I was going there anyway; I was simply curious about his opinion. He thought Tassajara was one of the most beautiful places in the world to practice, but that some of the longtime practitioners there "had dead eyes."

I could imagine what he might be referring to (the studiedly serious "I am a Zen person and must behave accordingly" expression), so I asked him what he thought caused this illness. He answered, "I think American Zen students feel a need to worship their teachers, and that's unhealthy for both students and teachers. Here in Japan, a Buddhist priest is a very ordinary thing. No one expects us to be God."

Sometimes I don't like wearing my robes; I imagine they can create a feeling of separation for people who don't have them. I also don't like some of the projections that attend them. But I believe it's part of a priest's job to try to overcome these projections and perceptions of separation. People wear different clothes, but if I allow mine to represent "betterness," I misuse the robe's intention to symbolize humility and vow: the vow to be one with all beings.

In Bloomington I supported myself by helping international graduate students with their English speaking and writing. One, a Chinese Buddhist, liked to confide her romantic woes. Once I empathized, "Yes, I just hate when that happens." She looked shocked. "But I thought as a priest you would have transcended all that!" All what, exactly? Love? Anger? Disappointment? Emotion in general? Maybe transcended being human altogether? Nice work if you can get it. But it isn't to be had, not in this incarnation at least.

One of the reasons I don't think of myself as a bodhisattva, despite my vows, is that a bodhisattva is described as a person who could abide in nirvana but chooses not to, out of her great compassion for those still trapped in samsara. I can't take credit for renouncing a permanent nirvana option I've never had. Furthermore, I can't immediately think of anyone I know who qualifies as a bodhisattva under this exacting definition. As far as I can tell, most of us commute regularly between samsara and nirvana; I don't think we have any other choice. That's the nature of our life, moment by moment, moment within moment. It's also the nature of nirvana and samsara—the shores always shifting as the river flows on. Who could be just one thing? How fortunate that each thing is everything! Mary Oliver wrote, "There is only one question: how to love this world." I wholeheartedly agree—it may not be my only question, but it's the one that moves me most. For me, it's the fundamental bodhisattva question.

I do love Zen practice, and what I love most is that it changes lives. Living by vow changes lives. It has changed my life, and I've seen it change other lives. When I lived in Maine, I sat with some people and we discussed Okumura Rōshi's *Homeless Kodo* book, one chapter at a time. Most of us had never practiced before. Except for me, no one was wearing any special clothes, and we weren't in a temple; we sat in a living room overlooking a river that had once separated the two worlds of a mill town: where the workers lived and the owners resided.

I'd edited *Homeless Kodo* with my usual ambivalence about editing, but each week I witnessed its words transform people: smoothing family relationships, putting work challenges in perspective, and most of all, calming mindstorms. It was remarkable to see words having such tangible power in the world, since writers often feel we're shouting into the wind. As poet John Keats had inscribed on his tombstone, "Here lies one whose words were writ in water." Like many artists, he died young and poor, without any idea what his poems would mean to future generations. Bodhisattvas do not necessarily know they are bodhisattvas. Maybe they cannot know it, because then they would stop being it.

I had a student in Bloomington who was difficult to reach. I emerged from our lessons frustrated and doubting myself. "Maybe despite all these years, I'm just not a very good teacher." This was a truly dispiriting thought. I entertained it for a while before realizing: the fact that I never know whether I'm a good teacher, that I'm always questioning and trying to improve—to that extent only am I a good teacher.

Over the past decade, my practice has included editing Okumura Rōshi's writings. I love words, and precision, clarity, and grace with them. But to be effective, an editor's mind must be a problem-seeking mind, a critical mind. It's easy for me to read or listen to someone and glide past grammatical issues or awkwardness of phrasing, because what I'm listening for is the feeling and the meaning behind the words. That's my natural instinct, and it's pleasurable. But when I switch on editing mind, I'm forced to cross-examine each word and punctuation mark: Are you necessary? Are you the best choice? Do you belong here—are you in right relationship with your companions in this sentence and paragraph? Do you clarify or obscure the intended meaning? Is the meaning what I think? Am I making changes to help the reader, or to suit my own voice?

Thoughtful editing is a painstaking interrogation not only of form (everything on a page), but also of emptiness (everything not there that maybe should be), of the author, and of myself. When I finish, no matter how diligently people have worked on a manuscript, it's peppered with red, and I feel like a jerk. Editing is a process that is loving in its intention and goal, because the editor is trying to help the author's voice come through at its clearest and most beautiful, and help the reader hear that voice. But the process doesn't feel loving at the time, at least not to me as an editor. It feels like a long bodhisattva no.

Although I loved Maine and my community there, I had to leave when I got very sick. I came to live with a friend in California. At times my illness seemed hopeless enough that I considered putting myself out of my misery. Reverence for life is a crucial precept, but I've never interpreted it to mean we must maintain our lives at any cost. What kept me here was accepting the truth of impermanence, a reader's curiosity about how my story would go if left to its own unfolding, and the knowledge that at least one beloved person's life would never be the same if I checked out prematurely. I recently lost a close friend, and my heart felt the fraying of Indra's net when that jewel dropped from its place and became something else. As Uchiyama Rōshi said, when a person dies, a whole world dies with them. Not only their world, but parts of others' worlds.

I've noticed that as I grow older, the importance of sangha increases. Until recently I practiced at a small, beautiful temple with a friendly sangha. It reminded me fondly of Sanshinji. But then one of its leaders started harshly censuring members for mistakes, real or imagined. I found this behavior deeply troubling. I remembered the story of someone asking a teacher whether it was all right to kill a scorpion, and the teacher answering that it was all right only if you could do it without a trace of hatred in your heart.

In my understanding, Zen training isn't driven by anger. This is another quality of Okumura Rōshi's teaching that distinguishes him. In my earlier practice, I'd often seen priests and teachers cast angry looks at students who hit a bell at the wrong time or in the wrong way. This was one of my ways of sorting through teachers. If after decades of practice, a misplaced bell upset someone that much, I'd better learn from a different teacher.

Stumbling over a few words of the *eko* detonated the first angry explosion I saw at my previous sangha. I'd helped train the *dōan*, who was nervous about taking on the job because he feared he couldn't do it perfectly. But we needed someone to do it, and I told him that if he was worried about how he'd look or what people would say, then he was thinking like a performer, which made the service into a performance. But service isn't a performance; it's an offering. As long as such an offering is made with your whole heart, there's no way to do it wrong.

A young Muslim friend tells me Islam is very democratic. An imam isn't a priest or an intermediary between "ordinary" people and Allah, but merely someone dedicated to studying the scriptures. She was very disturbed by what happened at the temple and urged me to speak out about it. I considered whether and how to do that. Most people in the sangha weren't particularly bothered by the leader's outbursts, including the doan who'd been berated. In the end, I simply decided I couldn't stand there in my robes and implicitly support what felt to me like uncontrolled anger and abuse of power. Where you stand and who you stand with matters. Still, I was sad to leave the sangha; saying no just never feels as good as saying yes.

I'm currently contemplating a return to school for training in counseling, a bodhisattva activity I've been attracted to and feared in equal measure. In my twenties I had a one-day tenure as a volunteer at Planned Parenthood, counseling women who'd just received the results of their pregnancy tests. My first and final client was in tears. She was a migrant farmworker who had several children already and couldn't afford another. I couldn't think of anything useful to say; I murmured a few words, listened to her cry, and concentrated on not crying myself. After half an hour, she thanked me and left. I called my supervisor the next day and quit, explaining how useless I'd felt, and how I'd very nearly cried, which could hardly have been reassuring to the client. She told me that in fact my client had felt better after our session; it was the first time she had felt someone really listening to her.

What I experienced as failure became a *kōan* about help: what is it? Giving people what they need or what makes us feel good to give? What are our motivations? Are we helping to serve them, or to validate ourselves? What are the limits of one person's ability to help another? Are false assumptions or hidden judgments on either side hindering our efforts? Can we help someone without a trace of selfishness in our hearts?

I once read that therapists often assume they help people through their words and methodologies—Jungian, cognitive behavioral, whatever they trained to do. But the writer asserted that people are helped most not by what we say, but by who we are, and by the quality of our relationship with them.

So how do we become better bodhisattvas? We work on ourselves. Zazen, and especially sesshin, has been one of my ways of working on myself, of gathering my heart-mind, of remembering the difference between society's values and my vows, between so-called reality and the true nature of life. People are sometimes surprised that I still sit Antaiji-style sesshins monthly if I can, often at home. To me it feels very straightforward. I sat for long enough that sitting became a normal thing to do. Turning off my email and phone and not doing what's expected for a few days became acceptable, in my mind at least. I know I may not always be able to do this, so I do it while I can. Starting tomorrow in fact, so I must end this now, a writer's hardest task, after beginning.

Recently I heard a dharma talk at my new sangha. A friend from Tassajara, a priest, writer, and hospice counselor spoke of his challenges in meeting suffering, and how he returns to our practice when he feels himself overwhelmed by the cries of the world. Afterward someone asked, "Practice is great, but what are we supposed to do about all the suffering when we stand up?" With a rueful smile, my friend said, "I don't know." I really respected his answer. It takes bravery to say "I don't know" from the teacher's seat. And it's true. He can't know what she should do when she stands up, because the bodhisattva vow manifests uniquely according to each person's desires, abilities, and limits. Realizing our individual incarnation of a universal vow is the work of our lives. And vow isn't static; it's transformed along with the person who vows.

So if you ask me tomorrow what the bodhisattva vow means to me, I might give you a different answer. And that would be all right. I prefer questions to answers. Questions are alive. And every question worth its salt has as many answers as the ten thousand things.

AUTHOR BIOGRAPHIES

SHŌHAKU OKUMURA is the founder and abbot of Sanshin Zen Community and was born in Osaka, Japan, in 1948. In 1970, he was ordained by the late Kōshō Uchiyama Rōshi, one of the foremost Zen masters of the twentieth century. He received Dharma transmission from his teacher in 1975 and, shortly after, became one of the founding members of Pioneer Valley Zendo in Massachusetts. He returned to Japan in 1981 and began translating the works of Dōgen Zenji, Uchiyama Rōshi and other Sōtō masters from Japanese into English. In 1993, he moved back to the United States with his wife Yuko and their two children. He has previously served as teacher at the Kyōto Sōtō Zen Center in Japan and at the Minnesota Zen Meditation Center in Minneapolis, and was Director of the Sōtō Zen International Center in San Francisco for thirteen years. Today, Okumura Rōshi is recognized for his unique perspective on the life and teachings of Dōgen Zenji, derived from his experience as both practitioner and translator, and as a teacher in both Japanese and Western practice communities.

SHŌDŌ SPRING hosts the Mountains and Waters Alliance, plus a Zen permaculture farm and a small sitting group in southern Minnesota. She received dharma transmission from Okumura Rōshi in 2012, after studying with him, with Tenshin Anderson Rōshi, and originally with Dainin Katagiri Rōshi. In 2013 Shōdō organized and led the Compassionate Earth Walk, a 3-month spiritual walk along the proposed Keystone XL route through the Great Plains. She is a grandmother, a psychotherapist, an environmental activist, and the author of *Take Up Your Life: Making Spirituality Work in the Real World.*

DENSHŌ QUINTERO is the abbot of Daishin Temple and the head priest of the Sōtō Zen Community of Colombia in Bogota. He started practicing in 1984 and received monk ordination in France in 1987. In 1989, he founded a center for the diffusion and practice of Sōtō Zen in Bogota. In October 2001 he reordained at Antaiji with the abbot, Shinyu Miyaura. After Miyaura Rōshi's death in February 2002, he became a student of Okumura Rōshi and received dharma transmission from him in 2009. He is the translator of *Opening the Hand of Thought* by Kōshō Uchiyama Rōshi into Spanish and the author of two books, *Conciencia zen (Zen Consciousness)* and *El despertar zen: el camino de un monje colombiano (Zen Awakening: The Path of a Colombian Monk)*.

CENTRE SHIKANTAZA was founded in 1996 in the heart of Mons, Belgium by Mokushō Michel Deprèay, a student of Okumura Rōshi. The center is dedicated to the teaching and practice of Zen Buddhism in the tradition of the Sōtō school. It has been a member of the Belgian Buddhist Union (UBB) since 2003. It maintains links with all its members, but also with other Belgian and foreign associations and has created a partnership with the French association Mountains and Forests of Zen, founded by Joshin Bachoux Sensei.

EIDŌ REINHART is a a home care physical therapist who started practicing Zen in the seventies with Dainin Katagiri Rōshi at Minnesota Zen Meditation Center (MZMC). In 1993 she met Okumura Rōshi when he was the interim teacher at MZMC. She was ordained by him in 2006 and received transmission in 2015, and participated in two *ango* in Japan, one in 2013 and one in 2016. She lives in Minneapolis and practices with local sanghas as well as at Sanshin several times a year. Soon to be a grandmother for the first time, she has two adult sons and a daughter-in-law who live nearby, as well as four rescue cats, two of which were born during the spring *ango* she spent at Tōshōji in Okayama, Japan.

DŌJU LAYTON grew up in the Washington D.C. area. He received a Bachelor of Arts in German studies from the College of William and Mary and a Master of Science in evolutionary biology from the University of Missouri-St. Louis. While pursuing a Ph.D in biology, he began to feel dissatisfied with his direction and panicked at the thought of having no viable alternative. In 2011 he found himself at the Missouri Zen Center in St. Louis in the process of figuring out how to cope with this problem. There he practiced with Rosan Yoshida and found that through his zazen practice he was content to go with the flow and not worry so much about the future. Upon reading Kōshō Uchiyama's *Opening the Hand of Thought* and finding its presentation of Zen to be the most clear and straightforward he had encountered, in 2015 he moved to Sanshinji in Bloomington, with the aim of becoming a priest under Uchiyama's disciple, Okumura

Rōshi. Dōju was ordained as a novice priest in 2017. Unable to fully abandon academia, the following year he accepted an offer to begin a master's program in religious studies at Indiana University, where he will study Japanese Buddhism.

SHŌRYU BRADLEY was ordained as a Sōtō Zen priest in 2002 by Seirin Barbara Kohn at Austin Zen Center, and in 2004 he moved to Bloomington to study with Okumura Rōshi and the Sanshin Zen Community. He has also trained at Tassajara Zen Mountain Center in California and at Sōtōshu International Training Monastery *ango* held in the US and Japan. In 2010 he received dharma transmission from Okumura Rōshi. He holds a B.S. in psychology from Texas A&M University, an M.Ed. in Rehabilitation Counseling from the University of Texas at Austin, and is a candidate for certification in Japanese psychology at the ToDo Institute of Vermont. He is currently working to establish Gyōbutsuji, a mountain practice center offering monthly sesshins in the style of Okumura Rōshi and Kōshō Uchiyama Rōshi.

HŌKŌ KARNEGIS was named vice-abbot and successor at Sanshin in 2016. She previously served for three years as communications director at Hokyoji Zen Practice Community in southern Minnesota and for two years as interim practice director at Milwaukee Zen Center. She also served as an adjunct instructor at Lakeland College in Sheboygan (WI) where she taught Eastern Religious Traditions in the classroom and online. In 2005 she was ordained as a novice by Okumura Rōshi and received dharma transmission in 2012. She has spent time in several training temples in Japan, is recognized by Sōtōshu as *nito kyoushi* (second-rank teacher) and as a practitioner of *baika*, a type of Japanese Buddhist hymn created by Sōtōshu in 1952. She has a B.A. in Speech Communication/Broadcast from the University of Minnesota, and in 2009 completed an interdisciplinary master's degree there with a thesis on organizing and and leading the American sangha.

SHŌJU MAHLER was born in Paris and met Zen Buddhism in the United States, where she lived for many years. She was ordained by Dai-en Bennage Rōshi in 1999 and lived, practiced and studied for four years at Mount Equity Zendo in Pennsylvania. She also practiced for six months at the Aichi Senmon Nisōdō in Nagoya, Japan under the direction of Abbess Shundō Aoyama Rōshi. In 2005 she became Okumura Rōshi's disciple and practiced and studied at Sanshin under his guidance six months a year from 2005 to 2009, when he gave her dharma transmission. She is the founder and teacher of Zendo L'eau Vive in France.

KAIKYO ROBY, PhD, CT holds an undergraduate degree in Social Communication and a Doctorate in Sociology of Communication (1985) from the Sorbonne. She also received an integral dance education and for several years was dedicated to creating and teaching dance in Europe. She first ordained in the Sōtō Zen tradition in France in 1995 and then again with Okumura Rōshi in the United States, from whom she received dharma transmission. Her training included six months at the Aichi Senmon Nisōdō in Nagoya, Japan. A psychoanalyst, grief therapist and specialist in Pastoral Clinical Education, since 2003 she has worked as a hospice chaplain and she collaborated with a multidisciplinary team to write and publish the text *End-of-Life Care*. In addition to translating Buddhist texts into Spanish, she is the spiritual guide for three sanghas in Venezuela and one in Germany.

JŌKEI WHITEHEAD studied comparative literature at Harvard University and has worked mostly as a writer, editor, and English teacher. After training at Tassajara Zen Mountain Center, she has studied with Okumura Rōshi for the past decade and was ordained by him in 2011. She edited his book *The Zen Teaching of Homeless Kodo* and writes a blog at *polishingthemoon.com*.

Printed in Great Britain
by Amazon